VALUE

VALUE

Michael Allingham

St Martin's Press   New York

ISBN 0–312–83611–2

Library of Congress Cataloging in Publication Data

Allingham, Michael.
  Value.

  Bibliography: p.
  Includes index.
  1. Value.   I. Title.
HB201. A556   1982   338.5′21   82–6018
ISBN 0–312–83611–2   AACR2

To Daniel and Chloe, 2 May 1982

Contents

Preface   xi

1   INTRODUCTION   1
1. An interpretation   2. Ten questions   3. Walras'
contribution   4. Later developments   5. A plan of the book

2   COMMODITIES   5
1. The question   2. Commodities   3. Prices
4. Uncertainty   5. Contingent commodities
6. Commodity bundles

3   AGENTS   10
1.The question   2. Agents   3. Preferences   4. Properties of
preferences   5. Indifference curves   6. Utilities   7. Smooth
preferences   8. Scale-independent preferences   9. An
example   10. Endowments   11. Planned exchanges   12. A
second example   13. Contingent exchanges
14. Equilibrium   15. A third example

4   SOCIETY   21
1. The question   2. Optimal allocations   3. Incompleteness
of criterion   4. Incompleteability of criterion   5. Equilibria
and optima   6. Optima and equilibria   7. Smooth
preferences   8. An example   9. Non-convex preferences

5   COALITIONS   32
1. The question   2. Core allocations   3. An example
4. Equilibria and the core   5. Replication defined   6. Equal
treatment   7. The core and equilibria   8. Approximation
9. Non-replicated economies   10–11. Two further examples

6   PRICE-TAKING   41
1. The question   2. Manipulation   3–5. Three examples

6. Obtainable prices   7. Obtainable and equilibrium prices
8. Approximation   9. Non-replicated economies   10. A
further example   11. A lacuna

7   EXISTENCE   49
1.The question   2. An indirect approach   3. Excess
demands   4. Properties of excess demands   5. An example
6. A direct approach   7. Linear preferences   8. A second
example   9. Concave preferences   10. A third example
11. Large economies   12. Approximation   13. Non-replicated
economies

8   CONTINUITY   59
1. The question   2. Excess demands and attributes
3. Similar attributes and similar excess demands   4. Similar
excess demands and similar attributes   5. Non-critical
economies   6. Rareness of critical economies

9   UNIQUENESS   68
1. The question   2. Non-critical economies   3. Representative
economies defined   4. Uniqueness in representative economies
5. Multiple-market economies defined   6. Existence and
uniqueness confirmed   7. Non-representative economies

10   STABILITY   77
1. The question   2. The adjustment mechanism
3. Representative economies   4. Possibility of instability
5. Stability confirmed   6. Non-representative economies
7. Local stability   8. Disequilibrium exchanges

11   PREDICTION   86
1. The question   2. Shifts in demand   3. Representative
economies   4. Possibility of perverse changes   5. Prediction
confirmed   6. Non-representative economies   7. The
substitutes case defined   8. Uniqueness and stability with
substitutes   9. Prediction with substitutes

12   CONCLUSION   95
1. A summary   2. Production   3. Capital   4. Money   5. An
assessment

13   APPENDIX   99
1. Value and scarcity   2. Scarcity and value

Bibliography
1. Historical references   2. General references   3. Specific   102
references

Index   104

Preface

The time has come Walras has said
To speak of many things.
Lewis Carroll, pseudonym of Dodgson,
quoted by Samuelson, mistranslated by
Kudryavtsev and retranslated by
Gerschenkron.

Pure economics is, in essence, the theory
of the determination of prices under a
hypothetical regime of free competition.
Leon Walras, translated by Jaffe.

Why is wheat more valuable than oats? In this monograph I propose an answer to this question, namely that wheat is more valuable than oats because it is scarcer, and then examine a number of questions which must in turn be answered to justify this.

The interpretation of value which I consider is that of 'the amount for which a thing can be exchanged'. Accordingly, I focus on the theory of value in exchange, and abstract from the problems of production, capital and money.

The discussion is intended to be rigorous without being technical. By this I mean that formal mathematical arguments are avoided entirely, but that the more informal arguments used in their stead are intended to be sufficiently precise as to be capable of being formalised without too much difficulty. This means that no understanding of mathematics is required to follow the argument; strictly speaking, no understanding of economics is required either, though some general familiarity with the language of the subject should prove useful.

My aim is to present the theory of value in a simple and unified framework, rather than to extend the theory; any such extensions that may be encountered are purely incidental. Thus any novelty there may be in this book is in the framework and arguments employed, rather

than in the results obtained from these. In the light of this aim I have
drawn on the work of a number of writers without individual
acknowledgement, though my more specific debts are indicated in the
bibliography.

The book is divided into chapters, and each chapter into sections;
sections are numbered consecutively within chapters. Figures and
examples are also labelled consecutively within chapters; when
referred to outside the chapter in which they occur their labels are
followed by the number, in parentheses, of the section in which they
are to be found. Symbols are only used when to avoid doing so would
be particularly cumbersome; in such cases it is a straightforward, if
sometimes lengthy, matter to express the argument purely verbally.
Where symbols are employed Latin letters (x, p and so forth) represent
simple numbers, such as the quantity or price of wheat, and Greek
letters, (α, λ and so forth) compound entities, such as commodity
bundles or price combinations.

The material of the book may be used as the basis of a series of
lectures to graduate or advanced undergraduate students, and indeed I
have used it as such at the London School of Economics and the
University of Kent. I am grateful to students and colleagues at these
and other institutions for many helpful discussions, and particularly
so to John Craven, Charles Kennedy and John Whitaker for com-
menting on the manuscript.

1 Introduction

1. Value, according to the Oxford dictionary is 'the amount ... for which a thing can be exchanged'; in other words, value is the price which prevails in the market, or equilibrium price. In this book I discuss what determines value in this sense, or, to be more concrete, why wheat is more valuable than oats (bushel for bushel).

The interpretation and answer I propose to give to this question are as follows. Consider an economy consisting of a number of agents, each of whom has some given amounts of wheat and oats. Each agent also has a view of the usefulness of these commodities to him, a view which is represented by his being able to specify, given any two bundles of wheat and oats, which bundle he prefers. Now assume that some price of wheat in terms of oats is announced, say 2 bushels of oats per bushel of wheat. On the basis of this, together with his given endowment of and preferences between wheat and oats, each agent plans exchanges, some planning to acquire wheat in return for oats and some oats in return for wheat. It may be that at this ratio the total amount of wheat which agents plan to acquire is more, or indeed less, than the total amount they plan to surrender, in which case the price of wheat may be expected to rise, or indeed fall. However, if at this price the total amounts of wheat which agents plan to acquire and surrender are the same, and this also applies for oats, then this price may be expected to prevail in the market, and thus be an equilibrium price, reflecting the relative values of wheat and oats.

It follows that the values of things, or their equilibrium prices, are determined by the degree to which they are considered useful and on the amounts in which they are available, that is to say on the degree to which they are 'scarce'. Thus wheat is more valuable than oats (bushel for bushel) because it is scarcer.

2. To justify this answer I propose to examine the following ten questions:

   Commodities: What are commodities and how are they exchanged?

Agents: What are agents and how do they plan exchanges?

Society: Does society as a whole accept the market mechanism?

Coalitions: Do all coalitions in society accept the market mechanism?

Price-Taking: Do all agents take market prices as given?

Existence: Do equilibrium prices exist?

Continuity: Do equilibrium prices depend continuously on the attributes of the economy?

Uniqueness: Are equilibrium prices unique?

Stability: Are equilibrium prices stable?

Prediction: Do equilibrium prices depend in a predictable way on the attributes of the economy?

These questions fall into three groups: the first two questions define a framework for the discussion, the next three provide a justification for focusing on equilibrium prices, and the final five analyse the properties of such prices.

3. The theory of value in a full equilibrium sense originates with Leon Walras, and indeed continues to be dominated by his work. Born in 1834, Walras first studied engineering, but soon gave up his studies to turn to literature, living somewhat precariously as a novelist. His interest in economics was aroused when he was 23, by his father, who encouraged him to spend the following 12 years studying the subject. When 35, Walras achieved some recognition, being appointed to a chair at Lausanne, where he remained, although retiring from his chair when he was 57, until his death at the age of 75 in 1910. While at Lausanne he completed his canonical work, the *Elements of Pure Economics*. This was first published in French in 1874, and subsequently revised three times to appear finally as a posthumous definitive edition in 1926. This latter edition, which formed the basis of Walras' non-technical summary, also published posthumously, in 1938, was translated into English in 1954.

Walras had no formal instruction in economics, but received substantial guidance from his father. He did, however, read widely, and was familiar with the theories of value of Smith and Ricardo, which he criticises as being too concerned with the availability of things, and of Say, which he criticises as being too concerned with their usefulness. The recognition that the theory of value must combine these two forces, and the construction of this theory, is unmistakably due to Walras.

In assessing Walras' work I shall not attempt to do better than to quote from Schumpeter's definitive 1954 *History of Economic Analysis* (page 827; all references are to editions cited in the bibliography):

> So far as pure theory is concerned, Walras is in my opinion the greatest of all economists. His system of economic equilibrium, uniting as it does the quality of 'revolutionary' creativeness with the quality of classic synthesis, is the only work of an economist that will stand comparison with the achievements of theoretical physics. Compared with it, most of the theoretical writings of that period – and beyond – however valuable in themselves and however original subjectively, look like boats beside a liner, like inadequate attempts to catch some particular aspect of Walrasian truth.

Walras' *Elements* defined a framework in which to examine the concept of value, thus answering the questions of commodities and agents. It also posed the questions of existence, uniqueness, stability and prediction, and prepared the groundwork for answering these, though stopped short of producing complete answers.

4. Walras' work was first taken up by his pupil Pareto, who in his *Manual of Political Economy* (1906; translated from the Italian in 1971), discussed the question of society. At approximately the same time Edgeworth, in his *Mathematical Psychics* (1881), discussed the related question of coalitions. The questions of stability and prediction were taken up in Hicks' *Value and Capital* (1939), though the former was posed in a somewhat restricted way. The basic logical question of existence, and also the question of uniqueness, were examined rigorously by Wald in a series of papers in the 1930s, summarised in 1936 (translated from the German in *Econometrica* in 1951). Wald's work on existence, together with that of Pareto on society, was extended by Arrow and Debreu in the 1950s, this work culminating in Debreu's *Theory of Value* (1959).

Debreu's book, in which, in the words of the author (page viii), 'the theory of value is treated ... with the standards of rigor of the contemporary formalist school of mathematics', marks the coming of age of Walrasian theory, a day when, in Walras' words (translation, page 48), 'mathematical economics will rank with the mathematical sciences of astronomy and mechanics, [and] justice will be done to our work'.

The years of maturity since Debreu's *Theory of Value* have seen the questions of price-taking and continuity being raised, as well as substantial extensions and refinements to the answers to other questions, particularly those of coalitions, uniqueness, stability and prediction. This work is too recent to be placed in perspective, and indeed is still developing rapidly. I shall make no attempt to identify its key components here, though refer to many of these in the bibliography.

5. The aim of this introductory chapter is to present the problems and place these in their historical context. In the following ten chapters I take up the ten questions raised here, while in a final chapter I disucss some extensions and draw some conclusions.

My purpose in this book is to examine the relation between equilibrium price and scarcity, rather than to provide a justification for interpreting value as equilibrium price and thus establishing a relation between value and scarcity. However, I present a translation of Walras' discussion of this relationship in an appendix.

Finally, references and suggestions for further reading are presented in a bibliography.

2 Commodities

1. I shall start by enquiring what commodities are and how they are exchanged. This must be discussed before more substantive questions about the value of commodities can be considered.

To answer this question I first explain what things are to be considered as commodities, how these are distinguished from one another, and how their prices are to be defined. I then discuss the problems raised by time and uncertainty, and show how these may be avoided if commodities are interpreted as being contingent. I conclude by explaining what is meant by a commodity bundle, and the value of this.

The answer to this question is mainly a matter of definition. However, the definitions proposed are coherent, and also relate well to reality on the whole, although the treatment of uncertainty is somewhat artificial.

2. Commodities are those things that are scarce, that is both useful and available only in limited amounts. Thus neither waste, which though limited in availability is not useful, nor water, which though useful is available in (effectively) unlimited amounts, are commodities. On the other hand, goods such as wheat, services such as labour and assets such as land are all commodities; such things are both useful and available only in limited amounts.

Commodities are distinguished from each other not only on the basis of their obvious physical nature, including quality, but also by the place and time at which they are available. Thus not only is wheat distinguished from labour, and hard wheat from soft, but also wheat at the farm is distinguished from that at the granary and wheat available today is distinguished from that available tomorrow. Quantities of each commodity are measured in some given units, for example wheat in bushels, labour in hours and land in acres.

The essence of the theory of value may be seen most clearly in the context of pure exchange. Accordingly, I shall abstract from the problem of production, that is the transformation of some commodities into others, such as wheat into flour. This means that I must also abstract from the problem of capital, that is produced means of production, such as mills. Further, I shall abstract from the problem of money, that is an intrinsically worthless medium of exchange, such as pound notes. Thus for the most part I assume that commodities are available in given amounts and are exchanged for each other directly (though in Chapter 12 I consider the effect of incorporating production, capital and money). More technically, and as an approximation, I also assume that there are only a finite number of commodities, which means that individuals' horizons must be limited, and that these are perfectly divisible, which means that individuals can exchange half a cow as readily as a whole cow.

3. The price of wheat in terms of oats, given the units of measurement of wheat and oats, is the amount of oats which can be obtained in exchange for a bushel of wheat. The price of oats in terms of wheat is of course the inverse of this: if 2 bushels of oats can be obtained in exchange for 1 of wheat then ½ bushel of wheat can be obtained in exchange for 1 of oats. Since it does not matter which price we use I shall, for consistency, always consider price as being that of wheat in terms of oats unless I indicate otherwise, and take the units of measurement as given.

4. Although some commodities may only be available in the future I shall consider all exchanges as being made today, and thus interpret these as exchanges of contracts to deliver commodities rather than as physical exchanges of commodities themselves. For example, an individual could acquire wheat to be delivered tomorrow, or future wheat, by exchanging contracts today to deliver oats today, or spot oats, in return for the delivery of wheat tomorrow. He could also achieve the same end indirectly by today exchanging spot oats for future oats and then tomorrow exchanging the oats thus acquired, which would then be spot oats, for then spot wheat. Provided that he is certain about the furture there is no reason for his taking this indirect route, so that all exchanges may be considered as being made today, and the future may be collapsed into the present.

However, the individual may well be uncertain about some aspect of the future, such as the weather, which will affect his planned exchanges. This may be either because it affects the usefulness or availability of wheat or oats to him directly, or because it affects the usefulness or availability of wheat or oats to others, and thus the price at which he can exchange oats for wheat with others. In this case whether he exchanges spot oats for future wheat directly, or exchanges spot oats for future oats and then waits until tomorrow, when the weather will be known, before exchanging then spot oats for wheat, will depend on his, and others', expectations about the weather. In this case the future cannot be collapsed into the present.

5. This problem may be avoided if we extend the way in which commodities are distinguished, so that they are contingent on the state of nature. By such a state I mean a complete specification of everything that may affect the usefulness or availability of commodities to anyone, such states being defined in such a way that exactly one must occur. For purposes of illustration I shall assume that there are only two states, say sun and rain. Then wheat (that is hard wheat available at the farm tomorrow) to be delivered if there is sun (tomorrow) will be distinguished from wheat to be delivered if there is rain.

Just as with any other commodity, the price of wheat-if-sun in terms of spot oats is the quantity of oats which must be delivered today in return for the promise to deliver a bushel of wheat tomorrow if there is sun tomorrow (and nothing if there is rain). Certain commodities may be constructed by combining these contingent commodities. Thus a bushel of future wheat may be acquired with certainty by acquiring a bushel of wheat-if-sun together with a bushel of wheat-if-rain; of course the price of certain future wheat is the sum of the prices of wheat-if-sun and wheat-if-rain.

If there are active markets for all contingent commodities an individual could acquire wheat-if-sun in exchange for spot oats directly; alternatively, he could do this indirectly by today exchanging spot oats for oats-if-sun and then tomorrow, if there is sun, exchanging then spot oats for wheat, while if there is rain doing nothing. Provided that he is certain about the effect of sun, that is about all aspects of tomorrow given that there is sun, then again there is no reason for his taking the indirect route, and all exchanges may be considered as being made today. Since 'sun' is a complete specification of everything which is relevant there is no more difficulty in this case than in the case of complete certainty, that is where there is only one possible state of nature.

In practice, active markets for all contingent commodities may well not exist, if only because there would need to be many of them. If there were n simple commodities, such as wheat, and m states of nature, such as sun, there would need to be nm contingent commodities, such as wheat-if-sun. Fortunately, we may achieve effectively the same result if we only have active markets for one simple commodity contingent on all states of nature, together with spot markets both today and tomorrow. This reduces the necessary number of markets from nm to $2n + m$, that is m contingent markets and n spot markets both today and tomorrow. This is more realistic: it may not be possible in practice to acquire either wheat-if-sun or oats-if-sun, but it may well be possible to acquire general insurance against drought.

In this case, where there are only contingent markets for oats, say, an individual can no longer acquire wheat-if-sun in exchange for spot oats directly, but must do this indirectly by today exchanging spot oats for oats-if-sun and then tomorrow, provided there is sun, exchanging then spot oats for wheat. Since the result of these indirect exchanges is precisely that of the direct exchange when there were markets for all contingent commodities, when we could consider all exchanges as being made today, we may in this case effectively do the same. Tomorrow's exchanges are still *determined* today; the only difference is that with contingent commodities they are *effected* tomorrow rather than today.

There does remain a practical problem with contingent commodities, which is that the price of spot wheat in terms of oats which will rule tomorrow provided there is sun cannot be observed today, as it could in the case where there were markets for wheat-if-sun and oats-if-sun. Instead, this must be calculated, but since 'sun' is a complete specification of everything relevant this should be possible.

6. In the light of this I shall assume that commodities are defined so that the future may be collapsed into the present, and so does not need to be considered explicitly. Most of the theory of value can be discussed perfectly satisfactorily in the context of a single-market economy, that is one with only two commodities, and I therefore propose to do this, at least until it becomes unduly restrictive. Following Walras, I will refer to these commodities as 'wheat' and 'oats', with their qualities, locations, dates and states of nature remaining implicit.

I shall refer to a combination of given amounts of these two commodities, say x bushels of wheat and y of oats, as a commodity bundle. The value, in terms of oats, of such a bundle is the amount of oats which can be obtained by exchanging this bundle, each component at a time, for oats. If the price of wheat, in terms of oats, is p

then px bushels of oats can be obtained for the x bushels of wheat, while of course y bushels of oats can be obtained for the given y bushels, so that the value of the bundle is $px + y$.

3 Agents

1. Given the nature of commodities I now enquire what agents are and how they plan exchanges. Again, this must be discussed before more substantive questions about value in exchange can be considered.

To answer this question I first explain how agents and their preferences are to be interpreted. I then discuss the properties of agents' preferences in detail, and show that these together with agents' endowments determine agents' planned exchanges. I conclude by noting when such exchanges are compatible, and thus when a price is an equilibrium price.

The answer to this question is mainly a matter of definition. However, the definitions proposed are coherent, and also relate well to reality; given these definitions there are no problems in specifying agents' planned exchanges, and when these are compatible.

2. Agents are any entities in the economy which plan exchanges. These may be individuals, families, communes, or any similar groups. Each agent has given preferences about wheat and oats, and is endowed with given amounts of these commodities. The economy is thus defined by the preferences and endowment of each of its agents. I shall start by discussing preferences, then consider endowments, and then show how these together determine planned exchanges.

3. An agent's preferences concern bundles of wheat and oats, but only feasible bundles, that is those with positive or zero quantities of each commodity. Such bundles may be illustrated geometrically, as shown in Figure 3A, where the horizontal distance from the origin to a point such as α represents the amount of wheat contained in the bundle α and the vertical distance the amount of oats. (Unless indicated otherwise all such L-shaped figures are to be interpreted in this way.)

Preferences are defined by the specification, given any two bundles α and β, of whether α is preferred to β, β is preferred to α, or α and β are considered indifferent to each other. This specification must

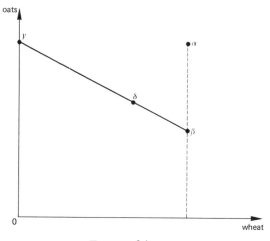

FIGURE 3A

have some consistency: exactly one of these three possibilities must apply, any bundle must be considered indifferent to itself, and if α is considered indifferent to β then β must be considered indifferent to α. Further, preferences must be transitive, in that if α is preferred to β and β is preferred to some third bundle γ then α must be preferred to γ, and similarly for indifference. Preferences have three further properties, which I shall discuss at more length.

4. The first property is that preferences are continuous, that is change only slowly as bundles change: if α is preferred to β then α is preferred to all bundles sufficiently close to β. This would not apply, for example, in the case where bundles were judged solely on the amounts of wheat they contained, unless this was the same in each when the amount of oats would be taken into account, with more always being preferred to less. In this case the bundle α in Figure 3A containing 2 bushels of each commodity would be preferred to the bundle β containing 2 bushels of wheat and 1 of oats, but bundles very close to β, for example all those containing $2 + h$ bushels of wheat and 1 of oats when h is positive but very small, would be preferred to α. However, this counter-example is somewhat unrealistic, and the property is reasonable.

The second property is that preferences are monotone, or that more is preferred to less: if α contains more of each commodity than β, or more of one and the same amount of the other, as in Figure 3A, then α is preferred to β. There are many examples where this may not apply, but if commodities can be disposed of then less cannot actually be preferred to more: if after a point more wine is unpleasant it can be poured away. Thus the property is not unreasonable.

The third property is that preferences are convex, or that mixtures are preferred to extremes: if β and γ are considered indifferent, as is assumed in Figure 3A, then any combination of these, such as δ, is preferred to either β or γ. By a combination of two bundles β and γ I mean a bundle containing some fraction h of the quantities of each commodity contained in β and the fraction $1 - h$ of those contained in γ; this may be illustrated by a point such as δ lying on the line joining β and γ. Again, this property may not always apply: for example, a bottle of claret may well be considered indifferent to one of burgundy while either is preferred to half a bottle of each. Despite this the property is not too unreasonable, and I will generally assume that it applies, though will from time to time consider the effects of relaxing it.

5. Preferences may be illustrated by indifference curves. To derive these consider some bundle α, as shown in Figure 3B, draw some (upward-sloping) ray through the origin, and note the bundles β and γ on this ray which contain the same amounts of wheat and oats respectively as α. Because of monotonicity β is preferred to α and α is preferred to γ. Then because of continuity there is some bundle between β and γ on the ray which is considered indifferent to α, and because of monotonicity there is only one such bundle, say δ.

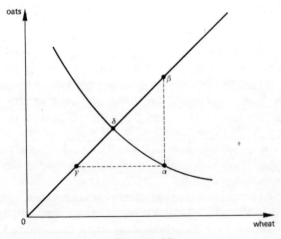

FIGURE 3B

Repeating this procedure for all possible (upward-sloping) rays produces a locus of all the bundles considered indifferent to α (other than any on the axes), as shown in the figure. This locus is the indifference curve through α. If this is done for all possible bundles, or even all bundles along any upward-sloping ray, a complete indifference curve map is obtained, as illustrated in Figure 3C. Because of monotonicity distinct indifference curves never meet, and bundles on curves further from the origin are preferred to those on lower indifference curves; for the same reason indifference curves are downward sloping. Provided that convexity applies indifference curves will be convex to the origin, as are the upper two in Figure 3C, but without convexity this need not be the case, and curves may have shapes such as that of the lower curve in this figure.

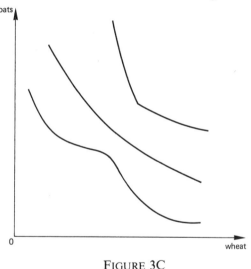

FIGURE 3C

6. A more concise way to represent preferences is to assign a number to each bundle in such a way that if α is preferred to β then it is assigned a higher number, and if α is considered indifferent to β then they are both assigned the same number. This assignation of numbers may be made in many ways. One method is to define the number assigned to a bundle α as the distance from the origin to the point β where the indifference curve through α cuts the diagonal ray through the origin; this is illustrated in Figure 3D. These numbers are known as utilities, though as they may be assigned in many ways they have no meaning beyond that of a numerical representation of preferences.

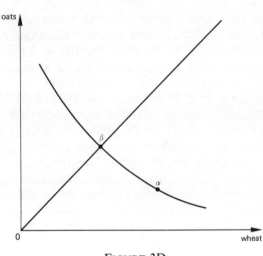

FIGURE 3D

7. An interesting class of preferences is that of those which are smooth. Such preferences are represented by indifference curves that have no corners, so their slopes at any point (that is the slopes of the tangents at these points) are well-defined; in Figure 3C the lower two indifference curves have this property but the upper curve does not. If preferences are smooth then the slope of the indifference curve at some point represents the amount of oats which the agent would be prepared to forego to obtain a (small) unit increase in his amount of wheat. This is his rate of substitution of wheat for oats, and represents his own valuation of wheat in terms of oats. If preferences are smooth they may be defined by specifying the rate of substitution at each bundle.

8. Another interesting class is that of preferences which are scale-independent (sometimes known as homothetic). Indifference curves representing such preferences have the same slope irrespective of how far they are from the origin. This means that, provided the rate of substitution is defined, it is the same at all points along any given ray. Equivalently, the rate of substitution at any bundle depends only on the ratio of the amount of wheat to that of oats contained in the bundle, and not on the absolute amounts of each. Such preferences are illustrated in Figure 3E. If preferences are both smooth and scale-independent they may be defined by specifying the rate of substitution on each ray. This is illustrated by the following example.

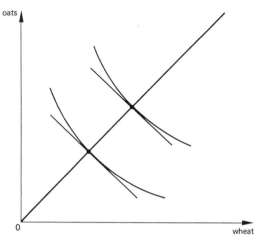

FIGURE 3E

9. *Example 3A.* Preferences are defined by assigning to a bundle containing x bushels of wheat and y of oats the utility level xy. Indifference curves are thus defined by the locus of points for which $xy = c$ for various (positive) values of c, that is by rectangular hyperbolas, as illustrated in Figure 3F. It is straightforward to show that, provided x and y are both positive, these preferences are continuous, monotone and convex, and also that they are smooth. (These properties may not apply if either x or y is zero, but this need not concern us here.)

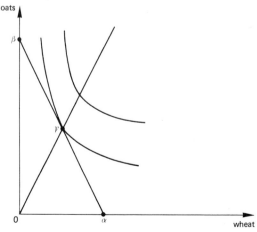

FIGURE 3F

I shall show that these preferences are scale-independent by demonstrating that the rate of substitution (between wheat and oats), say s, at a bundle containing x bushels of wheat and y of oats is equal to the slope of the ray through this bundle, say r, that is to y/x.

Draw the line shown in Figure 3F connecting the bundles α, containing 2 bushels of wheat only, and β, containing 4 bushels of oats only. This is the locus of points for which $2x + y = 4$; its slope is 2. The point γ, where this line is tangential to some indifference curve, will be on this line and on an indifference curve, and will thus uniquely satisfy the equations for each, that is $2x + y = 4$ and $xy = c$ respectively. Combining these two equations gives $2x + c/x = 4$ at the point γ. If $c = 2$ this condition is satisfied at one point, where $x = 1$, but if c exceeds 2 the condition cannot be satisfied at all while if c is less than 2 it will be satisfied at two points. Thus the point γ must be that where $x = 1$, and so where $y = 2$ and $r = 2$. Thus at the point γ both s and r are equal to 2, so that $s = r$.

Using the same argument we may see that any line with a slope of 2, however far from the origin, meets an indifference curve where $r = 2$, so that s is always equal to r when $s = 2$. Repeating this procedure for different values of s shows that $s = r$ everywhere, as claimed.
(The notation used in this, and following, examples is continued in subsequent examples without further comment.)

10. I now turn to endowments, which limit the bundles an agent can obtain through exchange. Each agent takes the price ratio as given, and can only make exchanges in this ratio. If the price of wheat in terms of oats is p and he plans to acquire (or surrender) x bushels of wheat then he must plan to surrender (or respectively acquire) px bushels of oats. Thus the value of the bundle he plans to acquire must be the same as that of his endowment, or equivalently, the net value of his exchanges must be zero.

This is illustrated in Figure 3G, where his endowment bundle is α: the bundles he can obtain through exchange are those on the downward sloping line through α with slope p, known as his budget line. Each agent is endowed with a positive amount of at least one commodity, so that the budget line is well-defined at any price. Strictly speaking, an agent could also obtain bundles underneath his budget line, providing he may dispose of commodities, but because of monotonicity he would never plan to do this.

11. The exchange which an agent plans, given the price ratio, is the best, according to his preferences, of those available to him. This will

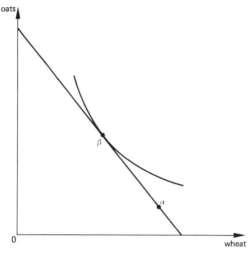

FIGURE 3G

be the bundle where his budget line meets the highest indifference curve it encounters, that is to say is tangential to an indifference curve, as is the case at the bundle β in Figure 3G. There will always be some best bundle, and provided that preferences are convex there will be only one such. This is because if there were two best, and therefore indifferent, bundles on the budget line then any bundle between them on this line would be available, and because of convexity preferred to either of them.

If preferences are smooth and the agent's planned bundle is positive (that is contains positive quantities of both commodities) then the slope of his indifference curve will be the same as that of his budget line. This means that his rate of substitution, or personal valuation, is the same as the price ratio, or market valuation.

This explanation assumes that neither commodity is free, that is that the price ratio is neither zero nor infinite. If, wheat, say, were free then each agent could acquire as much wheat as he wanted without surrendering any oats; because of monotonicity he would therefore plan to acquire an infinite amount of wheat. However, I do not consider this further, since such a plan could never be achieved, given that there is only a finite amount of wheat available in the economy.

Note that a small change in price leads to only a small change in an agent's planned exchanges, as is illustrated in Figure 3H. In the same way a small change in an agent's endowment or in his preferences also leads to only a small change in his planned exchanges.

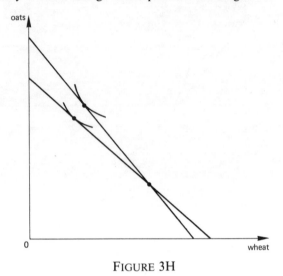

FIGURE 3H

A agent's planned exchanges are illustrated by the following example.

12. *Example 3B.* The agent's preferences are those of Example 3A, and his endowment bundle contains 2 bushels of wheat only. Since any bundle containing a zero amount of either commodity yields a zero utility level while any positive bundle yields a positive utility level he will only plan to obtain positive bundles. (This means that the failure of some of the preference properties for bundles with zero quantities of some commodity noted in Example 3A is immaterial.)

As preferences are smooth and a positive bundle is planned at any (regular, that is positive and finite) price p we must have $s = p$. Since with these preferences $s = r$ this means that, if his planned bundle contains x bushels of wheat and y of oats, then $p = r = y/x$. The ratio of the amount of oats he plans to acquire, that is $y - 0$, to that of wheat he plans to surrender, that is $2 - x$, must be p, so we also have the condition that $y - 0 = p(2 - x)$. These two conditions together determined the planned bundle as $x = 1$ and $y = p$.

More generally, if his endowment bundle contains a bushels of wheat and b of oats then the same argument determines his planned bundle as $x = (pa + b)/2p$ and $y = (pa + b)/2$.

13. This explanation of how planned exchanges are determined

applies in a formal sense whether commodities are taken as being contingent or not. The interpretation, however, is somewhat different in the contingent commodities case.

Preferences now incorporate beliefs about the likelihood of the various states of nature occurring and attitudes towards risk, as well as preferences between simple commodities. Consider the case where the two commodities are now wheat-if-sun and wheat-if-rain instead of wheat and oats. At any bundle containing c bushels of each commodity, that is any bundle which gives c bushels of wheat with certainty, the rate of substitution, if defined, reflects the agent's belief about the relative likelihood of sun and rain. For example, if he considers sun to be twice as likely as rain he will require $2h$ bushels of wheat-if-rain to compensate him for the loss of h bushels of wheat-if-sun (for small values of h), so that his rate of substitution of wheat-if-sun for wheat-if-rain will be 2.

Given this, the properties of continuity and monotonicity have no essentially new implications. However, the property of convexity does have the additional implication that the agent is averse to risk, in the following sense. If he considers sun and rain to be equally likely then he will be indifferent between a bundle containing 2 bushels of wheat-if-sun only and one containing 2 bushels of wheat-if-rain only, but because of convexity he will prefer a bundle containing 1 bushel of each to either of these. This third bundle gives him 1 bushel of wheat with certainty, while each of the other bundles give him either 2 bushels or nothing, so on average give him 1 bushel, but with some risk. Thus he is averse to risk in that he prefers a certain bundle to an otherwise equivalent risky bundle.

The other determinant of the agent's planned exchange, that is his endowment, and thus his budget line, has no new interpretation. The values of both his endowment and his planned bundle are known with certainty; indeed, all exchanges may be considered as being made today.

14. At any given price some agents may plan to acquire wheat and others to surrender wheat, and there is no reason why the total amount agents plan to acquire should be the same as the total amount they plan to surrender. If these quantities are not the same then planned exchanges are incompatible, and the price may be expected to change. However, if at some given price these quantities are equal (and the corresponding quantities for oats are also equal) then all planned exchanges are possible, and the price may be expected to

prevail and thus be an equilibrium price, reflecting the relative values of wheat and oats. In the case where all agents' preferences are smooth and they all plan positive bundles each agent's rate of substitution, or subjective valuation, will be the same as the equilibrium price, or objective value; values are then agreed unanimously. This is illustrated by the following example.

15. *Example 3C*. The economy has two agents, who I shall refer to as Leon and Karl, each with the preferences of Example 3A. Leon's endowment contains 2 bushels of wheat only, and Karl's 2 bushels of oats only.

Using Example 3B we have $s = p$ for each agent, so that each agent has the same s and thus the same r. If Leon has x bushels of wheat and y of oats then Karl must have $2 - x$ bushels of wheat and $2 - y$ of oats, as the total availability of each commodity is 2 bushels. Since they have the same r this means that $y/x = (2 - y)/(2 - x)$, so that $y/x = 1$ and thus $p = r = 1$. Thus the (unique) equilibrium price in the economy is 1, as is each agent's subjective valuation.

The same result could also be obtained using Example 3B by noting that at price p Leon plans to have 1 bushel and Karl $1/p$ bushels of wheat. These plans will be compatible if their total is the same as the total amount of wheat available, that is if $1 + 1/p = 2$, that is if $p = 1$ (the corresponding condition for oats is also satisfied at $p = 1$). Of course the same result may also be seen immediately by symmetry.

More generally, if the total availability of wheat and oats are a and b bushels respectively the same argument shows that the (unique) equilibrium price is b/a, regardless of the distribution of the commodities between the agents.

4 Society

1. Given the nature of commodities and agents I now enquire whether society as a whole accepts the market mechanism. This will only be the case if the allocation of commodities which society as a whole receives under the market mechanism is better, in some sense, than any other possible allocation. This is a first requirement for equilibrium prices to be relevant.

To answer this question I first discuss the sense in which one allocation is better for society than another, and provide a justification for this interpretation. I then explain what is meant by an equilibrium allocation, and show that every equilibrium allocation is optimal, in that there is no better allocation, and also show that every optimal allocation may be obtained as an equilibrium.

The answer to this question is quite satisfactory. There is an unambiguous correspondence between equilibrium and optimal allocations, so that society as a whole may be expected to accept the market mechanism.

2. An allocation for the economy is a specification of the bundle each agent receives. These bundles must together be feasible, in that the total amounts of each commodity allocated to the agents must be the same as the total amounts available, that is the total endowments. Strictly speaking, amounts allocated could be less than those available, but because of monotonicity this would clearly be undesirable and is therefore ignored. For the time being I shall assume that there are only two agents, Leon and Karl. We may then represent allocations geometrically in the box of Figure 4A; this is known as an Edgeworth box, though in fact is due to Pareto. The length of the box represents the total availablity of wheat, that is the sum of Leon's and Karl's endowment of wheat, and the height of the box the total availability of oats.

A point in the box such as α represents the allocation which gives the bundle α as seen in the usual way, that is from the south-west corner of the box, to Leon, and as seen from the opposite origin, that

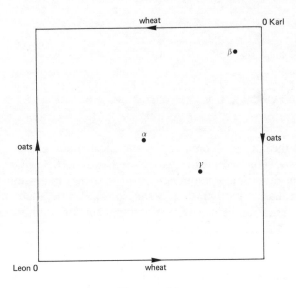

FIGURE 4A

is the north-east corner, to Karl. Thus the amount of wheat received by Leon in the allocation α is represented by the horizontal distance from the west side of the box to α, and that received by Karl by the distance from the east side of the box to α; the amounts of oats received by each agent are represented by the corresponding vertical distances. (All such box-shaped figures are to be interpreted in this way.)

An agent prefers an allocation α to an allocation β if he prefers the bundle he receives in α to that he receives in β, and is indifferent between the two if he is indifferent between the bundles he receives in each. Following Pareto, I will define an allocation α to be better for society than an allocation β if every agent prefers α to β, or if at least someone prefers α to β and everyone else is indifferent between the two; α is equivalent for society to β if every agent is indifferent between α and β. An allocation is optimal if there is no better allocation for society, that is if any move away from it makes someone worse off. This Pareto criterion is an ethical judgement, but one which seems acceptable.

3. The problem with the Pareto criterion is not that it is objectionable, but that it is incomplete: if Leon prefers β to α and Karl prefers α to β, as would be the case in Figure 4A, the criterion does not

specify which allocation is better for society, nor even that they are equivalent. This means that there may be many optimal allocations. The criterion may be made complete by extending it in such cases where it says nothing; this may be done in various ways.

One possible way is to specify, in this case, that α is better than β because Karl prefers α. However, this introduces an unwarrantable asymmetry in the agents, and indeed makes Kare a dictator, in that society's choices always reflect his preferences whatever the views of the rest of society.

A second possibility is to specify that β is better than α because it is nearer the north-east corner of the box. However, this introduces an unwarrantable asymmetry in the allocations, in that it makes judgements based on irrelevant factors, that is factors other than the preferences of the agents between α and β (note that Leon will not always prefer allocations which are nearer the north-east corner).

Yet a third possibility is to specify that α and β are equivalent. The problem with this is that it may make society's views intransitive. Using this extension α would be equivalent to β, and because of monotonicity β would be equivalent to the allocation γ in Figure 4A; but it may well be that both agents prefer α to γ, so that α is better than γ.

It seems reasonable in extending the Pareto criterion to ensure that, at the very least, these problems of dictatorship, irrelevance and intransitivity are avoided. Again this is an ethical judgement, but one which seems acceptable.

4. Perhaps surprisingly, it is impossible to extend the Pareto criterion in this way. To show this, which is a form of a result known as Arrow's theorem, I shall construct cases where the three properties of non-dictatorship, relevance and transitivity lead to a contradiction, thus showing that the avoidance of the three problems of dictatorship, irrelevance and intransitivity in all cases is impossible. In doing this I shall use the assumptions of non-dictatorship and transitivity explicitly, and that of relevance implicitly, that is in making judgements only on the basis of agents' preferences.

I shall first show that if some set of agents is decisive over some pair of allocations α and β then this set is decisive over any other pair of allocations, say γ and δ. By the set being decisive over α and β I mean that α is deemed better than β whenever all the agents in this set prefer α to β and all other agents (if any) prefer β to α. Consider the case where all the agents in this set rank the four allocations in the order γ,

α, β, δ and all the other agents in the economy (if there are any) rank these in the order β, δ, γ, α. Then γ is better than α and β is better than δ because of the Pareto criterion, while α is better than β because the set is assumed to be decisive over α and β; because of the assumption of transitivity these together mean that γ is better than δ. Since everyone in the set prefers γ to δ and everyone else prefers δ to γ this means that the set is decisive over γ and δ. Thus if a set is decisive over some pair of allocations it is decisive over all pairs. This argument assumes that α, β, γ and δ are all distinct; similar arguments apply if this is not the case.

I shall next show that, not surprisingly, if some set of agents is decisive, that is if society always reflects the view of its members when they disagree with the other agents, then society always reflects their view whatever the preferences of the other agents. To see this assume that some set is decisive and consider the case where all agents in this set rank three allocations in the order α, β, γ and all other agents (if any) rank β above both α and γ but may have any preferences between α and γ. Then α is better than β because the set is decisive, and β is better than γ because of the Pareto criterion; because of transitivity these together mean that α is better than γ. Since everyone in the decisive set prefers α to γ, and α is better than γ whatever the preferences of the other agents between α and γ, the result follows.

I now show the contradiction. Because any individual agent would be a dictator if he were decisive there are some nondecisive sets, for example those consisting of only one agent. Take some non-decisive set, and consider the case where all the agents in this rank three allocations in the order α, β, γ, some individual agent not in this set ranks these in the order γ, α, β and all other agents (if there are any) rank them in the order β, γ, α. The only agents who prefer α to γ are those in the set, so if α were better than γ the set would be decisive; thus γ is better than or equivalent to α. Similarly, β is better than or equivalent to γ, because the individual agent is non-decisive. Because of transitivity these together mean that β is better than or equivalent to α. This in turn means that the enlarged set consisting of all the agents in the original set together with the individual agent is non-decisive, since everyone in this set prefers α to β and everyone else prefers β to α. Repeating this argument eventually shows that the set consisting of all the agents in the economy is non-decisive, which contradicts the Pareto criterion.

It follows from this that there is no satisfactory way of extending the Pareto criterion; since this criterion is acceptable as far as it goes we are justified in using the concept of optimality which it implies.

5. The optimal allocations for the economy may be illustrated geometrically. To do this first draw indifference curves for both Leon and Karl, as in Figure 4B. Provided that preferences are convex, Leon's indifference curves will be convex to the south-west corner, with preference increasing as we move north-east, while Karl's indifference curves will be convex to the north-east corner, with preference increasing as we move south-west. Now take any indifference curve for Leon, draw the highest indifference curve for Karl which meets this, and note the point where the curves meet. There will be one and only one such point for each of Leon's indifference curves; it may be a point in the interior of the box, such as α, where the indifference curves are tangential, or one on the boundary, such as β. This point will represent an optimal allocation since any move away from it will place at least one agent on a lower indifference curve, that is make someone worse off.

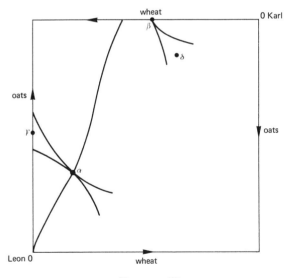

FIGURE 4B

The curve in Figure 4B connecting all points where indifference curves are tangential, such as α, and then following the edges of the box, through points such as β, to the two origins is known as the contract curve. It is clear that all allocations on the contract curve are optimal. Indeed it is also the case that no allocation which is not on the contract curve can be optimal. This is because, starting from any allocation not on the contract curve, such as γ or δ, we can make both agents better off by moving to an allocation on the curve, such as α or β, respectively. It follows that the set of optimal allocations consists of all allocations on the contract curve.

Equilibrium allocations may also be represented in the box; these are allocations in which each agent's bundle is the one he plans at equilibrium prices. In Figure 4C the endowment allocation, that is the allocation in which each agent's bundle is his endowment bundle, is α. The downward-sloping line through α with slope equal to the price ratio is the budget line for Leon; it is also the budget line for Karl. Given this price Leon will plan the bundle β, where his indifference curve is tangential to this line, while Karl will plan the bundle γ, where his indifference curve is tangential to the line. (Strictly speaking, β is an allocation not a bundle; however, I use the phrase 'Leon will plan the bundle β' to mean that Leon plans the bundle he receives under the allocation β, and so forth.) In this case these two plans are incompatible, because Leon plans to acquire more oats than Karl plans to surrender. Thus the price is not an equilibrium one.

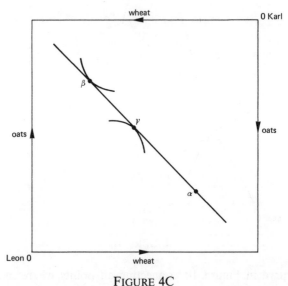

FIGURE 4C

However, in Figure 4D, where again the endowment allocation is α, the prices associated with both the budget lines shown are equilibrium prices. In the case of the flatter line both agents plan the bundle (they receive under the allocation) β, and in the case of the steeper line both plan γ; in each case these plans are compatible, and both β and γ are equilibrium allocations. This discussion makes it clear that all equilibrium allocations are on the contract curve, and thus are optimal.

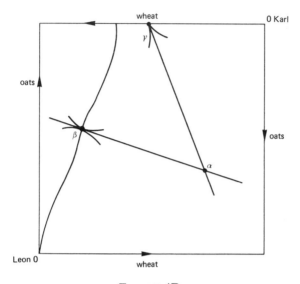

FIGURE 4D

This result, that every equilibrium allocation is optimal, is known as the first theorem of welfare economics. It may be seen more directly as follows. If each agent preferred some allocation α to an equilibrium allocation β then the value at the equilibrium price associated with β of the bundle he received in α would be greater than that of his endowment bundle; if it were not then he would have planned α rather than β. This means that the total amount of at least one commodity received under α would be greater than its availability, so that α would not be feasible.

6. Note that the set of equilibrium allocations depends on the endowment allocation, unlike the set of optimal allocations, which is independent of endowments. The first theorem simply says that an equilibrium allocation for any given endowment is optimal. To justify the market as an allocation mechanism I must also show that any optimal allocation may be obtained through the market, given the appropriate endowment allocation.

Since any optimal allocation is on the contract curve we may always draw a downward sloping line through such an allocation, such as α in

Figure 4E, with the property that all allocations preferred to α by Leon lie above this line and all those preferred to α by Karl lie below it. This means that if the endowment allocation were at any point on this line, such as γ, the slope of the line would represent an equilibrium price and α would be an equilibrium allocation, given the endowment γ. Exactly the same argument can be used if the optimal allocation is a point on the boundary of the box, such as β.

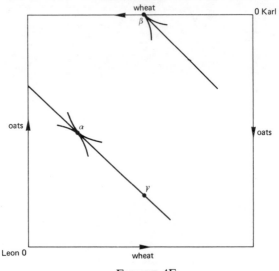

FIGURE 4E

This result is the second theorem of welfare economics: any optimal allocation may be obtained as an equilibrium allocation, given the appropriate endowment allocation.

These two theorems together imply that society has no need to look beyond the market mechanism, but they do not imply that society never will do this. For example, any given optimal allocation could in principle be obtained by centralised planning as well as in this decentralised way through the market. This would be extremely cumbersome in practice, though the redistribution of endowments required for the decentralised market alternative might also be difficult.

7. In the case where each agent's preferences are smooth, and we restrict our attention to allocations in the interior of the box, optimal allocations are those where each agent has the same rate of substitu-

tion. For example, if Leon's rate of substitution (of wheat for oats) were 2 while Karl's were ½ they would both benefit by Leon acquiring some (small) amount of wheat from Karl in exchange for the same amount of oats. Thus optimal allocations are those where each agent has the same subjective valuation. Also, in this case, equilibrium allocations are those where each agent's rate of substitution is the same as the price ratio.

The first theorem thus applies because if each agent's rate of substitution is the same as the common price ratio then each agent must have the same rate of substitution. The second theorem applies because if each agent has the same rate of substitution we may always choose a price ratio equal to this. Thus the equivalence, in this sense, between equilibrium and optimal allocations is explained by the equivalence between subjective valuation and price, or objective valuation. This equivalence is illustrated by the following example.

8. *Example 4A.* Each agent has the preferences of Example 3A (3.9). Consider the following allocations:

	Leon		Karl	
	wheat	*oats*	*wheat*	*oats*
α	2	0	0	2
β	1	1	1	1

The endowment allocation is α, so that the economy is that of Example 3C (3.15); the equilibrium price is therefore 1 and the equilibrium allocation β. This is an optimal allocation because each agent has the same r, of 1, and thus the same s.

We may also see that α is an optimal allocation by noting that, with these preferences, any bundle preferred to a bundle δ containing c bushels of each commodity must have the property that the total number of bushels it contains, that is the number of bushels of wheat added to that of oats, say t, exceeds $2c$. This is illustrated in Figure 4F, where bundles preferred to δ lie above the indifference curve through δ, and thus above the downward-sloping line through δ with slope equal to the indifference curve slope at this point, that is $s = r = 1$; but this line is the locus of all bundles with $t = 2c$, so all bundles above this line have t greater than $2c$. Using this property, any bundle preferred by Leon to β must have t greater than 2, and similarly for Karl. Thus in any allocation preferred by both agents to β the total number of bushels involved, that is Leon's t plus Karl's t, must exceed 4; this is impossible, as only 2 bushels of each commodity are available.

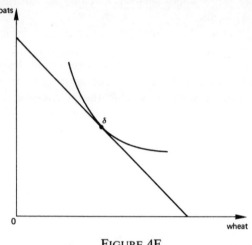

FIGURE 4F

The optimal allocations are those allocations where each agent has the same s, and thus the same r, that is those on the diagonal of the box, as illustrated in Figure 4G; this also follows from symmetry. The equilibrium allocation β, reflecting the equilibrium price of 1, is clearly an optimal allocation. Any optimal allocation, such as γ, may be obtained as an equilibrium using the same price ratio of 1, since at such an allocation $s = 1$ for each agent.

9. If preferences are not convex then an equilibrium allocation will still be optimal. This follows from the direct argument used in Section 4.5, which makes no reference to convexity.

However, optimal allocations may no longer be obtainable as equilibrium allocations. In Figure 4H, where the upper two indifference curves represent Leon's non-convex preferences and the lower curve represents Karl's convex preferences, the allocation α is optimal, but cannot be obtained as an equilibrium. No budget line through α would lead Leon to plan this bundle; for example, given the line shown he would plan the bundle β, though Karl would plan the bundle α.

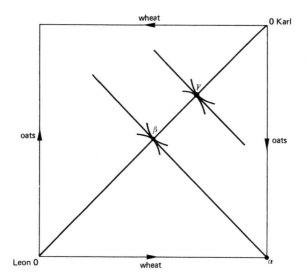

FIGURE 4G

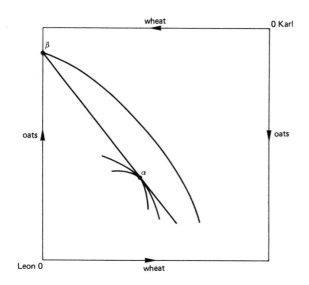

FIGURE 4H

5 Coalitions

1. Given that society as a whole accepts the market mechanism I now enquire whether all coalitions in society do likewise. This will be the case if the allocation which each possible coalition of agents receives under the market mechanism is better for the coalition than any other allocation it could obtain. This is a second requirement for equilibrium prices to be relevant; if may be seen as an extension of the first requirement, that society as a whole accept the market.

To answer this question I first examine the allocations which no coalition can improve on for itself, that is the core allocations, and show that every equilibrium allocation has this property, but that there may be core allocations which are not equilibrium allocations in a small economy. I then explain what is meant by a large economy, and show that in such an economy the only core allocations are equilibrium allocations.

The answer to this question is satisfactory in large economies, where equilibrium and core allocations are equivalent. However, this is not necessarily the case in small economies, where some coalitions may not accept the market.

2. A core allocation is an allocation which all sets of agents, or coalitions, accept, that is to say which no coalition can improve on. A coalition can improve on an allocation in this sense if there is some other allocation which is seen as being at least as good by each of its members, and actually better by some, and which the coalition can obtain from its own resources, that is by making exchanges only among its members.

In a two-agent economy core allocations may be illustrated as in Figure 5A, where the endowment allocation is α. In this case there are three possible coalitions: Leon alone, Karl alone, and Leon and Karl together. The only bundle which Leon alone can obtain is his endowment, so if Leon cannot improve on an allocation it must be one which he prefers to his endowment. The position for Karl alone is similar. If Leon and Karl together cannot improve on an allocation then by definition the allocation is an optimal one. Thus the set of core

32

allocations consists of the optimal allocations which are preferred, or deemed indifferent, to the endowment allocation by each agent, that is all those allocations on the contract curve lying between allocations γ and δ in Figure 5A. It is clear that there will always be some such allocations.

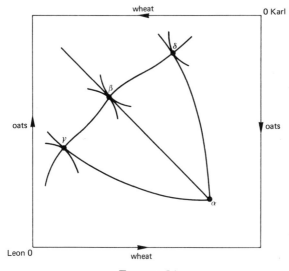

FIGURE 5A

If there are more agents then there are more possible coalitions to improve on any given allocation: if there are 3 agents there are 6 possible coalitions, and so forth. Thus in a sense there will be fewer core allocations when there are more agents. This is illustrated by the following example.

3. *Example 5A*. There are three agents, Leon, Karl and Maynard, each with the preferences of Example 3A (3.9). Consider the following allocations.

	Leon		Karl		Maynard	
	wheat	*oats*	*wheat*	*oats*	*wheat*	*oats*
α	4	0	4	0	0	8
β	4	4	2	2	2	2
γ	4	0	2	3	2	5

The allocation β is preferred to α, the endowment allocation, by each agent, and is also optimal, as each agent has the same r, of 1, and thus the same s, at β. However, β is not a core allocatiion, since the coalition consisting of Karl and Maynard could achieve γ by making exchanges only between themselves, and each of these agents prefers γ to β. Note that γ is not a core allocation either, since each agent does not have the same s, which means that it is not optimal.

4. Each agent must prefer any equilibrium allocation to the endowment allocation, unless he receives the same bundle in each, for otherwise he would plan to make no exchanges. Since any equilibrium allocation is also optimal it follows that any equilibrium allocation is a core allocation in a two-agent economy. This is illustrated in Figure 5A, where β is an equilibrium allocation.

In fact an equilibrium allocation is a core allocation however many agents there may be, as may be seen using the same argument as that which shows that any equilibrium allocation is optimal. If each agent in some coalition preferred an allocation α to an equilibrium allocation β then the value at the equilibrium price associated with β of the bundle he received in α would be greater than that of his endowment bundle; if it were not he would have planned α rather than β. This means that the total amount of at least one commodity received by the coalition under α would be greater than its availability to the coalition, so that the coalition could not obtain α.

The fact that all equilibrium allocations are core allocations does not in itself show that all coalitions will accept the price mechanism. To complete the demonstration I should also show that all core allocations are equilibrium allocations, that is show equivalence between core and equilibrium allocations. However, this is not always the case: for example in Figure 5A the core allocations γ and δ could not be equilibrium allocations, because of convexity. Indeed, we should not expect this to be the case in a two-agent, or other small, economy. In such economies all agents necessarily have some degree of monopoly power, which they may be able to exploit to obtain an allocation which they prefer to the competitive equilibrium allocation. This means that we may only expect equivalence between core and equilibrium allocations in economies where all agents have negligible monopoly power, which will necessarily be large ones.

5. The simplest way to interpret an economy becoming larger while at the same time retaining its original characteristics is through replication. The original two-agent economy is replicated by specifying a

four-agent economy in which two agents, which I shall refer to as type-L agents, have the same preferences and endowments as Leon has in the original economy, and two (type-K) agents the same preferences and endowments as Karl. Thus in Figure 5B the southwest origin, the indifference curves convex to that origin, and the allocation α as seen from that origin all relate to each type-L agent, and the same entities relative to the north-east origin relate to each type-K agent.

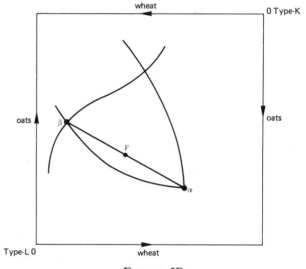

wheat

0 Type-K

oats

oats

Type-L 0

wheat

FIGURE 5B

6. We cannot represent all allocations of this replicated economy as single points in this Edgeworth box, but we can so represent all equal treatment allocations, that is all those in which all type-L agents receive the same bundle, as do all type-K agents. It is clear that equilibrium allocations have this equal treatment property. If two agents have the same endowment then at any given prices they have the same budget line, and if they also have the same indifference curve then they plan the same bundle. In fact this applies whether or not the price is an equilibrium.

If we are to demonstrate equivalence between core and equilibrium allocations we must show that core allocations also have this property. To do this, first assume that the type-L agents, say, receive different bundles but that these lie on the same type-L indifference curve. Then each type-L agent could obtain the average of these bundles, and, because of convexity, each would prefer this. Thus the coalition consisting of both type-L agents could improve on the original allocation, which could not then be a core allocation.

Now assume that one type-L agent receives a better bundle, according to the type-L preferences, than the other and consider the coalition consisting of this agent and the worse-off of the type-K agents, or either of these if they are equally well-off. These two agents control half the total endowments of the economy, so could each obtain half of the total of the bundles received by their respective types: that is, the type-L agent in the coalition could obtain the average of the two type-L bundles, and similarly for the type-K agent. Since the agents in the coalition are worse-off than those not in the coalition they are worse-off than the average of their types, and would therefore prefer these average bundles. Thus this coalition could improve on the original allocation, which could not then be a core allocation.

7. This result allows us to compare the set of core allocations in the original two-agent economy with that in the replicated four-agent economy, and to show that, as suggested, the core in the replicated economy is smaller than that in the original economy.

I first show that some allocation, in fact the allocation β in Figure 5B, which is a core allocation in the original economy, is not a core allocation in the replicated economy. To see this consider the allocation giving γ, the mid-point of the endowment allocation α and β, to each type-L agent, giving β to one type-K agent, and giving α to the other type-K agent. This is a feasible allocation because the common bundle received by each type-L agent, γ, is the same as the average bundle received by the two type-K agents, that is half of β plus half of α. The coalition consisting of both type-L agents and the first type-K agent can obtain this because it is feasible and leaves the only excluded agent, the second type-K agent, at his endowment. Finally, this coalition prefers this allocation to β because both type-L agents prefer it and the included type-K agent's bundle has not changed. This means that β is no longer a core allocation.

On the other hand, any core allocation in the replicated economy is certainly a core allocation in the original economy, since all coalitions in the former are coalitions in the latter, and if an allocation cannot be improved on by any coalition in the larger economy it cannot be improved on by any in the smaller.

We may continue to replicate the economy in the same way to

obtain any number of agents of each type. Loosely speaking, if we have infinitely many of agents of each type, in which case the economy is certainly large, then all core allocations are equilibrium allocations. More precisely, the only allocations which are core allocations for all replications of the economy are equilibrium allocations. Since we have seen that all equilibrium allocations are core allocations, whatever the size of the economy, this demonstrates the equivalence between core and equilibrium allocations in large economies, a result known as Edgeworth's conjecture.

To see this result first note that the equal treatment property applies to any number of replications, for the same reasons as apply for one replication. We may therefore interpret 'core allocations for all replications' in the same way as we may compare the sets of core allocations in the original and replicated economies.

Now note that core allocations must be optimal, and preferred, or considered indifferent, to the endowment allocation by agents of each type. I shall take any such potential core allocation which is not an equilibrium allocation, such as β in Figure 5C, and show that this is not in fact a core allocation for all replications of the economy.

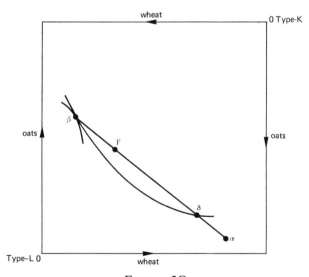

FIGURE 5C

The line from the endowment allocation α to β must intersect one of the indifference curves through β, here I assume the type-L's, say at δ; if it did not then either β would be an equilibrium allocation or the type-L agents would prefer α to β. Choose a whole number n, possibly very large, such that the allocation γ, which is the fraction $1/n$ of the distance from β to α, is between β and δ, as shown. Now take an economy in which there are n agents of each type, and consider the allocation giving γ to each type-L agent, giving β to each of $n-1$ type-K agents, and giving α to the remaining type-K agent. This is a feasible allocation because the common bundle received by each type-L agent, γ, is the same as the average bundle received by the type-K agents, that is the fraction $(n-1)/n$ of β plus $1/n$ of α. The coalition consisting of all type-L agents and the first $n-1$ type-K agents can obtain this because it is feasible and leaves the only excluded agent, that is the last type-K agent, at his endowment. Finally, this coalition prefers this allocation to β because all type-L agents prefer it and the included type-K agents' bundles have not changed. This means that β is not a core allocation for the replication with n agents of each type, and thus not a core allocation for all replications.

8. An economy with infinitely many agents is of course an abstraction, used to show the exact equivalence between core and equilibrium allocations when the monopoly power of each agent is truly negligible. It will be an informative abstraction only if this equivalence occurs approximately in large but finite economies, where the monopoly power of each agent is small but not negligible. By this equivalence occurring approximately I mean that if I specify any positive distance, however small, there will be some replication for, and beyond, which all core allocations are closer to some equilibrium allocation than this distance. Fortunately, this is the case, as follows directly from the result that the sets of core allocations get smaller as the economy grows, each set containing all the equilibrium allocations, together with the result that the only core allocations which exist when the economy is infinitely large are equilibrium allocations.

9. The reason why all core allocations are equilibrium allocations if there are many agents of each type is that each agent then has negligible monopoly power. If there were many type-L agents but only one type-K agent then the latter might have some real monopoly power, and we should not necessarily expect equivalence between core and equilibrium allocations. Thus size alone does not guarantee equivalence; we also need some balance between the numbers of agents of different types. Indeed, if we do not have this balance then core allocations may not have the equal-treatment property; since equilibrium allocations always have this property we should not then expect

equivalence between the two. These two problems, where an imbalance between the numbers of agents of each type leads to unequal treatment in a finite economy, and the lack of equivalence even with infinitely many agents, are illustrated by the following two examples respectively.

10. *Example 5B.* There are three agents, each with the preferences of Example 3A (3.9). Consider the following allocations.

	Leon		Karl		Maynard	
	wheat	*oats*	*wheat*	*oats*	*wheat*	*oats*
α	4	0	4	0	0	8
β	2	2	1	1	5	5

The endowment allocation is α, so that the economy is that of Example 5A. I shall show that β is a core allocation, even though it gives Leon twice as much of each commodity as Karl while Leon and Karl have identical preferences and endowments. Note that the allocation β is preferred to α by each agent, and is an optimal allocation because each agent has the same r, of l, and thus the same s.

The coalition consisting of Karl and Maynard cannot improve on β because, using the argument of Example 4A (4.8), any bundle preferred by Karl to β must have t greater than 2 and any bundle preferred by Maynard must have t greater than 10, so that the total number of bushels received by Karl and Maynard in any allocation they prefer to β must exceed 12; as they only have 4 bushels of wheat and 8 of oats between them they could not obtain such an allocation. Exactly the same argument shows that the coalition consisting of Leon and Maynard cannot improve on β. Finally, the coalition consisting of Leon and Karl cannot improve on β because any allocation they can obtain without making exchanges with Maynard must give each of them no oats and thus a zero utility level, while β gives each of them a positive utility level. It follows that β is a core allocation, as claimed.

11. *Example 5C.* There are $n + 1$ agents, Leon and some number n of type-K agents, each with the preferences of Example 3A (3.9). Consider the following allocations.

	Leon		Each type-K agent	
	wheat	*oats*	*wheat*	*oats*
α	$6n$	0	0	6
β	$4n$	$4n$	2	2
γ	$3n$	$3n$	3	3

The endowment allocation is α. The allocation β is not an equilibrium allocation: if it were then the price ratio would have to be equal to the common $s = r = 1$, and at such a price the value of Leon's bundle, $8n$, would exceed that of his endowment, $6n$. However, β is a core allocation, as I shall now show.

Note that β is preferred to α by each agent, and is an optimal allocation because each agent has the same r, of l, and thus the same s. Any coalition which could improve on β must contain Leon; if it did not then each of its members would receive no wheat and thus obtain a zero utility level. I assume therefore that such a coalition consists of Leon and some number k of type-K agents. Then using the argument of Example 4A (4.8) any bundle preferred by Leon to β must have t greater than $8n$ and any bundle preferred by each of the k type-K agents must have t greater than 4, so that the total number of bushels received by the coalition in any allocation it prefers to β must exceed $8n + 4k$. As the coalition only has $6n$ bushels of wheat and $6k$ of oats available, and as k cannot exceed n, the coalition could not obtain such an allocation. It follows that β is a core allocation. In fact the same argument also shows that any allocation lying between γ, which is an equilibrium, and β is also a core allocation.

It is clear that this lack of equivalence between core and equilibrium allocations applies whatever value n takes, that is however many agents there may be.

6 Price-Taking

1. Given that society as a whole and all possible coalitions accept the market mechanism I now enquire whether all agents take market prices as given. This will be the case if no agent is able to manipulate equilibrium prices to his advantage. This is a third requirement for equilibrium prices to be relevant; the first two requirements, that society as a whole and all coalitions accept the market justifies the market as an allocation mechanism, while this requirement justifies price-taking behaviour within this mechanism.

To answer this question I first explain how agents may attempt to manipulate prices to their advantage, and then show that, although they may succeed in this in small economies, the only prices they could obtain in large economies are equilibrium prices.

The answer to this question is satisfactory in large economies, that is where the market mechanism is accepted; in such economies prices are taken as given. However, this is not necessarily the case in small economies, where some agents may manipulate prices.

2. An agent is defined by his preferences and his endowment. He may therefore attempt to manipulate equilibrium prices to his advantage either by misrepresenting his preferences, which are unobservable, or by concealing some of his endowment, or even destroying this, though this would never be as beneficial as simply concealing it. As agents in a small economy necessarily have some degree of monopoly power we would expect them to be able to manipulate equilibrium prices to their advantage to some extent. That this is indeed the case is illustrated by the following three examples, where agents manipulate prices by concealing endowments, destroying endowments and misrepresenting preferences respectively.

3. *Example 6A.* There are two agents, each with the preferences of Example 3A (3.9). Consider the following endowments, and thus economies, each with its corresponding unique equilibrium price ratio, p, and equilibrium bundle received by Leon.

41

	Leon's endowment		Karl's endowment		p	Leon's bundle	
	wheat	*oats*	*wheat*	*oats*	–	*wheat*	*oats*
θ	4	0	0	4	1	2	2
ϕ	2	0	0	4	2	1	2

The equilibrium prices and bundles in these two economies are obtained using the results of Examples 3C (3.15) and 3B (3.12) respectively. If the true economy is θ and Leon conceals half his endowment the apparent economy is ϕ. The actual bundle Leon receives in the economy ϕ is his apparent equilibrium allocation given above together with the half of his endowment which he conceals; this actual bundle thus contains 3 bushels of wheat and 2 of oats. By concealing some of his endowment Leon can obtain more wheat than he obtains in the true equilibrium without losing any oats.

4. *Example 6B.* Each agent has preferences similar to those of Example 3A (3.9) except that they are defined by $s = r^3$ instead of by $s = r$. Consider the following economies, each with its corresponding equilibrium price and bundle received by Leon.

	Leon's endowment		Karl's endowment		p	Leon's bundle	
	wheat	*oats*	*wheat*	*oats*	–	*wheat*	*oats*
θ	20	0	0	10	1/8	4	2
ϕ	10	0	0	10	1	5	5

The equilibrium configurations in these two economies are obtained as follows. At an equilibrium of the economy θ we must have $s = p$ for each agent, so that each agent has the same $s = r^3$, and thus the same r. The same argument as used in Example 3C (3.15) then gives $y/x = 1/2$ and thus $p = t^3 = 1/8$; Leon's bundle is then determined by this and his budget requirement, $y - o = p\ (20 - x)$. The equilibrium of the economy ϕ is obtained in the same way. If the true economy is θ and Leon destroys half his endowment the apparent economy is ϕ. By destroying some of his endowment Leon can actually obtain more of each commodity than he obtains in the true equilibrium. Of course, if

Leon could conceal rather than destroy half of his endowment he would do even better.

5. *Example 6C.* The true economy is economy θ of Example 6A. The apparent economy differs from this in that Leon represents his preferences as being defined by $s = 3r$ instead of by $s = r$. At an equilibrium of this apparent economy we must have $s = p$ for each agent, but this s must be equal to $3r$ for Leon and to r for Karl. If Leon has x bushels of wheat and y of oats then Karl has $4 - x$ bushels of wheat and $4 - y$ of oats, so we have $3y/x = (4 - y)/(4 - x)$, which gives $y/x = 2/3$ and thus $p = s = 2$; Leon's bundle is then determined by this and his budget requirement, $y - o = p(4 - x)$. By misrepresenting his preferences Leon can obtain more wheat than he obtains in the true equilibrium without losing any oats.

6. We may only expect the ability of agents to manipulate prices to disappear in economies where all agents have negligible monopoly power, which will necessarily be large ones. As in the discussion of coalitions, I shall interpret a large economy as an economy with many agents of each type, and show that the ability to manipulate prices decreases as the number of agents of each type grows, eventually disappearing as this number becomes infinite. However, in contrast to the discussion of coalitions, I am now concerned with uncoordinated behaviour. I shall therefore consider the ability of an individual agent to manipulate prices given that all other agents act as price-takers; if no individual agent can do this then price-taking by all agents is to be expected.

I shall represent all types of manipulation, through misrepresentation of preferences or endowments or any combination of these, by, at any given price, letting one agent make an apparent planned exchange rather than his true planned exchange, that is the exchange determined by his true preferences and endowment. The manipulating agent may make any apparent exchange that is feasible; by this I mean that the value of the commodities which he plans to acquire must be the same as the value of those which he plans to surrender, and that he cannot plan to surrender more of a commodity than he is endowed with. For example, Leon's apparent exchanges in Examples 6A and 6B are the true exchanges of agents with different endowments, while in Example 6C his apparent exchange is the true exchange of an agent with different preferences. Note that an agent may always make his apparent exchange the same as his true exchange, since the latter is always feasible.

The object of making an apparent exchange is to obtain a more favourable equilibrium price, and thus a better bundle. Leon can obtain any price as an equilibrium price provided that the apparent exchange he must make to exactly balance Karl's true exchange at this price is feasible. This is illustrated in Figure 6A, where Leon can obtain the price represented by the steepest budget line by making his apparent planned bundle at this price balance Karl's true planned bundle, that is by making this α. However, Leon cannot obtain the price represented by the flattest budget line, where Karl's true planned bundle is β, because Leon's apparent planned bundle would also have to be β. This apparent bundle is not feasible because it lies outside Leon's axes, which means that it would require Leon to surrender more of one commodity, here wheat, than he is endowed with. Note that Leon can always obtain the true equilibrium price, that associated with the intermediate budget line, by making his apparent planned bundle the same as his true planned bundle, that is γ.

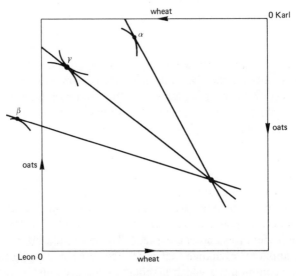

FIGURE 6A

The Edgeworth box in Figure 6A represents the true endowments. Leon can make the apparent box smaller by destroying some of his endowment, but as he is not constrained to make price-taking exchanges doing so would only restrict the prices he could achieve. Thus we are justified in considering only this true box.

7. If we replicate the economy we obtain an economy with four agents. Any allocation obtained as an apparent equilibrium has the

equal treatment property, for the same reasons as applied in Section 5.6, so we may continue to represent all relevant allocations in the original box. I shall use this to show that the set of prices which an agent can obtain in the replicated economy is smaller than that which he can obtain in the original economy.

I first show that there will be some prices which Leon can obtain in the original two-agent economy but which the first type-L agent cannot obtain in the replicated four-agent economy. This is illustrated in Figure 6B. In the original economy Leon can obtain the price represented by the budget line shown, where Karl's planned bundle is β, by making β his (Leon's) apparent planned bundle. However, in the replicated economy, where the price-taking type-L agent's planned bundle is α, both type-K agents' planned bundles are still β, so that the manipulating agent's apparent planned bundle would have to be γ, where γ is the same distance from β as β is from α. If he does this then the average bundle received by the type-L agents, that is half of γ plus half of α, is the same as the common bundle received by the type-K agents, that is β. However, γ is not a feasible planned bundle for the manipulating agent, as it lies outside his axes.

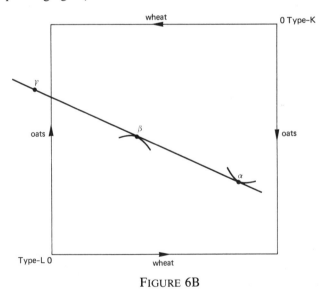

FIGURE 6B

On the other hand, all prices which the first type-L agent can obtain in the replicated economy can be obtained by Leon in the original economy. If the first type-L agent had been able to obtain the price shown in Figure 6B then γ would have lain within his axes. Since α

must lie within his axes because it is a true planned bundle and β is the mid-point of α and γ it follows that β must have lain within his axes, and thus been feasible. Thus in the original economy Leon could obtain this price by making β his apparent planned bundle.

If we continue to replicate the economy we may show that the only prices which an agent can obtain in all replications are the true equilibrium prices. This is illustrated in Figure 6C, where the endowment allocation is α and the budget line shown represents any price which is not a true equilibrium price. Because it is not a true equilibrium price the price-taking type-L agents' planned bundles, β, will not be the same as those of the type-K agents, γ.

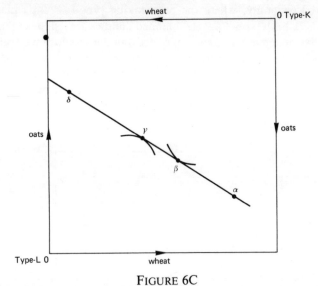

FIGURE 6C

If there are n agents of each type the apparent bundle planned by the manipulating agent to obtain this price must be δ, where the distance from δ to γ is n times that from γ to β. In this case the average bundle planned by the type-L agents, that is the fraction $1/n$ of δ plus $(n-1)/n$ of β, is the same as the common bundle planned by the type-K agents, that is γ. As the number of agents of each type increases the planned bundles β and γ do not change, so that δ must move further away from γ. If there are sufficiently many agents of each type then δ will move outside the relevant axes, and thus not be feasible, so that the manipulating type-L agent cannot obtain this price.

8. As in the discussion of coalitions, this result is only instructive if it

holds approximately in large but finite economies. By this holding approximately I mean that if I specify any positive amount, however small, there will be some replication for, and beyond, which all prices which any agent can obtain differ from an equilibrium price by less than this amount. This is in fact the case, as follows directly from the result that the sets of prices which any given agent can obtain get smaller as the economy grows, each set containing all the equilibrium prices, together with the result that the only prices which any agent can obtain if the economy is infinitely large are equilibrium prices.

We should also note that if the difference between the price an agent can obtain and the (assumed unique) equilibrium price is small then the difference between the bundle he receives under the two prices is small, so that he has no significant incentive to manipulate prices. This is because the bundle received by the manipulating agent is the difference between the total availability of commodities, which is fixed, and the total of the bundles received by the price-taking agents, and the latter bundles at the equilibrium price are similar to those at any prices close to the equilibrium price, as noted in Section 3.11.

9. For the same reasons as applied in the discussion of coalitions, size alone does not guarantee that no agent can manipulate prices; we also need some balance between the numbers of agents of different types. This is illustrated by the following example.

10. *Example 6D.* The economy is that of Example 5C (5.11). At the price of 2, using the results of Example 3B (3.12), Leon's planned bundle contains $3n$ bushels of wheat and $6n$ of oats, and each of the type-K agents' planned bundles contain $1\frac{1}{2}$ bushels of wheat and 3 of oats. These plans are not compatible, as they require $9n$ bushels of oats while only $6n$ bushels are available, so that this price is not an equilibrium price.

However, Leon can obtain this price as an equilibrium if all the other agents make their true plans by making his apparent planned bundle at this price that containing $4\frac{1}{2}n$ bushels of wheat and $3n$ of oats; all plans are then compatible. By so doing Leon can obtain more wheat than he would at the true equilibrium, where as noted in Example 5C (5.11) he has $3n$ bushels of each commodity, without losing any oats. It is clear that such manipulation is possible whatever value n takes, that is however many agents there may be

11. In this and the preceding Chapter 1 have examined two potential sources of deviation from price-taking behaviour in the market. In the preceding chapter this was through groups of agents not accepting the

market as an allocation system, while in the present chapter this was through individual agents manipulating prices within the market mechanism. There remain in principle two other potential sources of deviation: through individual agents not accepting the market, and through groups of agents manipulating prices. The first of these is of little consequence, as non-market actions necessarily involve some degree of cooperation, but the second may be important. The omission of a discussion of the problem of price manipulation by groups of agents constitutes a potential lacuna in the theory, though we may conjecture, using arguments similar to those developed in this and the preceding chapter, that this problem may be unimportant in large economies.

The pervasiveness of the possibility of price manipulation in small economies is a form of a result known as Gibbard's theorem, which is that under any allocation mechanism with the three properties of non-dictatorship, relevance and transitivity agents have an incentive to misrepresent their preferences. Gibbard's theorem may be established using arguments similar to those employed in Section 4.4 to prove Arrow's theorem; I shall not pursue this.

7 Existence

1. Given that equilibrium prices are generally accepted I now enquire whether such prices exist. This will be the case if there are always some prices at which all agents' planned exchanges are compatible; if this were not the case then the theory of value would be empty. This question may be illustrated by an analogy. Assume that we propose to interpret the weight of a lead ball as the equilibrium length to which it extends some given spring when suspended from it, that is the length at which the downward force of gravity on the ball balances the upward force of the spring, and that we propose to explain the weight of a ball by its diameter. This theory of weight would be empty if there were no such equilibrium length, that is if at any length the force of gravity were either greater or smaller than that of the spring.

To answer this question I first show that equilibrium exists in a simple case. I then explain the concept of excess demand and its properties, and use this to demonstrate the existence of equilibrium in general. Finally, I show that even if preferences are not convex equilibrium will always exist in large economies.

The answer to this question is quite satisfactory. Equilibrium prices always exist, given that preferences are convex; even if preferences are not convex equilibrium prices exist in large economies, that is those economies where such prices would be accepted.

2. I shall start by considering the simple case where preferences are smooth and such that any equilibrium allocation must lie in the interior of the Edgeworth box. This is illustrated in Figure 7A, where α is the endowment allocation. As noted in Section 5.4, any equilibrium allocation will be a core allocation, that is lie on the contract curve between β and γ, as shown. The slope of the budget line through β is less than the common indifference curve slope at β, because Leon's preferences are convex; similarly, the slope of the budget line through γ is greater than the common indifference curve slope at that allocation.

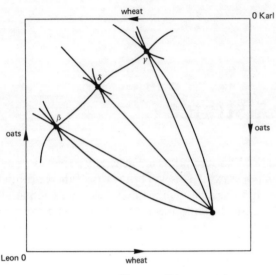

FIGURE 7A

Because preferences are continuous, and smooth, the common indifference curve slope changes only slowly as we move along the contract curve from β to γ. Also, if the budget line is rotated from that through β to that through γ its slope changes only slowly. Since the slope of the budget line is less than the common indifference curve slope at β and more than this at γ it follows that there is some intermediary allocation, say δ, at which these two slopes are the same. This is an equilibrium allocation, and the slope of the budget line through this is an equilibrium price.

The essence of this indirect approach involves finding planned exchanges, or an allocation, at which there is a balance between social valuation, or the common indifference curve slope, and price. Clearly this requires social valuation to be defined, that is preferences to be smooth and such that all core allocations are interior ones. On the other hand, the essence of the direct approach, to which I now turn, involves finding prices such that there is a balance in planned exchanges; this may be applied whether or not social valuation is defined. Before discussing this, however, I first develop the concept of excess demands.

3. The bundle which an agent plans to obtain through exchange at any given price is his demand bundle at that price, and his given endowment, which is independent of price, is his supply. Aggregate

demand and supply bundles in the economy are obtained by adding all
the agents' demand and supply bundles respectively, the difference
between these two being the economy excess demand bundle at the
given price. Thus excess demands are simply aggregate planned
exchanges, and if at some price the excess demand for each
commodity is zero then all planned exchanges are compatible, and the
price is an equilibrium.

The specification of the excess demand for each commodity at all
prices, which may be seen as the specification of excess demand curves
for each commodity, is completely determined by the attributes of the
economy, that is the preferences and endowments of the various
agents. Thus we may consider the economy as being defined by its
excess demand curve, rather than by its more primitive attributes, and
may consider an equilibrium price as one at which the excess demand
for each commodity is zero.

Finding such a price is easier than might appear because of a relationship known as Walras' law: at any regular (that is positive and
finite) price the value of excess demands is zero. This is because the
value of each agent's demand must be the same as that of his
endowment, or supply, so that the value of aggregate demand is the
same that of aggregate supply. Thus if the excess demands for wheat
and oats are x and y bushels respectively when the price is p then
$px+y=0$. This means that if x is zero then so is y, and conversely, so
that if the excess demand for one commodity is zero then so is that for
the other commodity. Because of Walras' law we may then consider
the (two-commodity) economy as being defined by just one excess
demand curve, say that for wheat.

4. Excess demand curves have various properties which derive from
the properties of the preferences and endowments which underlie
them. One such property is that the excess demand for wheat is
infinite when its price is zero. This is because monotonicity of
preferences implies that each agent's demand is infinite at zero price,
while given supplies are finite.

A deeper property is that of continuity, that is that excess demand
changes only slowly as price changes, so that excess demand curves
have no jumps. When price is positive (and finite) this is because each
agent's demand changes only slowly as price changes, as noted in
Section 3.11, while supplies do not change at all. There is a potential
problem when price becomes zero, because an agent endowed with x
bushels of wheat only will not be able to obtain more than x bushels of

wheat at any positive price, however small, yet when the price of wheat becomes zero he can, and will, plan to obtain an infinite amount. There will therefore be a jump in such an agent's demand when price is zero. However, this problem does not arise with any agent endowed with a positive amount of oats, and there must be some such agent. This means that some agent's demand, and thus agregate demand, increases without bound as price becomes zero, so that aggregate, and thus excess, demand is continuous at this price.

These two properties together imply that excess demand is positive at sufficiently low, but positive, prices. The same properties that apply to the relation between the excess demand for wheat and the price of wheat, say p, apply equally to the relation between the excess demand for oats and the price of oats, that is $1/p$. Thus the excess demand for oats is positive at sufficiently low, but positive, values of $1/p$, that is for sufficiently high, but finite, values of p. Because of Walras' law this means that the excess demand for wheat is negative at sufficiently high values of p, that is at sufficiently high prices.

The problem of possible discontinuties as price becomes zero is illustrated in the following example.

5. *Example 7A*. The economy is that of Example 3C (3.15). From the results of Example 3B (3.12) Leon's demand for wheat at any positive p is 1 bushel, while at zero p this is infinite, because of monotonicity. Thus Leon's demand is discontinuous at zero p.

However, Karl's demand for wheat at any positive p is $1/p$, so that aggregate demand is $1 + 1/p$, and excess demand $1/p - 1$. As p becomes zero this becomes infinite without any jumps, so that excess demand is continuous at zero p.

6. Excess demand curves may be represented geometrically, as in Figure 7B, where price is measured on the horizontal axis and excess demand on the vertical, the horizontal axis thus representing zero excess demand. (All such rotated-T-shaped figures are to be interpreted in this way.)

I use the properties of excess demand curves to show that equilibrium exists. Excess demand is positive, and thus above the horizontal axis, at sufficiently low price and negative, and thus below the axis, at sufficiently high price. Because the excess demand curve is continuous, that is has no jumps, it must therefore intersect the horizontal axis at some price, as shown. This price is one where the excess demand for wheat is zero, and thus, because of Walras' law, the excess demand for oats is also zero, and is therefore an equilibrium price.

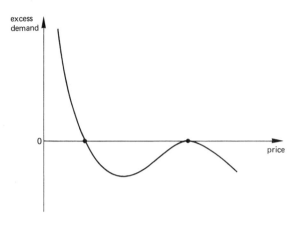

FIGURE 7B

7. I now consider the question of existence if preferences are not convex, and start with the intermediary case where some agent's indifference curves are not strictly convex, but do not have strict concavities either, that is where his indifference curves are linear (or, by extension, are convex apart from having linear parts).

This case is illustrated in Figure 7C, where the agent's indifference curves are lines, and his endowment is α. When price is equal to the constant slope of the indifference curve through α there are many bundles which the agent might plan to obtain. His demand bundle may be β, or α, or any bundle between these, and is not uniquely defined as it is when preferences are convex.

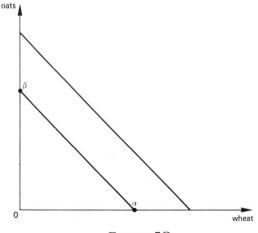

FIGURE 7C

This means that aggregate, and thus excess, demand is not uniquely defined at this price, so that the excess demand curve will have a vertical segment, as shown in Figure 7D. This curve still intersects the horizontal axis, so that an equilibrium exists, but if it does this in the vertical segment, as illustrated, this equilibrium will only be a potential, rather than a definite, equilibrium. This means that it will be a price at which all planned exchanges may be compatible, rather than one at which all planned exchanges will necessarily be compatible. At the price where the vertical segment occurs one agent has many possible planned exchanges; one of these will be compatible with the planned exchanges of other agents, but they cannot all be. This is illustrated in the following example.

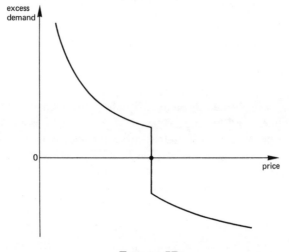

FIGURE 7D

8. *Example 7B*. The economy is that of Example 3C (3.15), except that Leon has linear preferences defined by $s = 1$ instead of by $s = r$; his indifference curves are thus the lines illustrated in Figure 7C. When $p = 1$ Karl's demand for wheat is 1 bushel, as in Example 3B (3.12), but Leon's is not uniquely defined: it may be zero or 2 bushels, that is at β or α respectively in Figure 7C, or any quantity between these. If in fact Leon's demand for wheat is 1 bushel then excess demand will be zero and the price will be an equilibrium, but if it is any other quantity then excess demand will be either positive or negative.

Note that no other price can even potentially be an equilibrium. If p

is less than 1 then Leon's demand for wheat is definitely 2 bushels and Karl's is positive, so that excess demand is positive. If p is greater than 1 then Leon's demand for wheat is definitely zero and Karl's is less than 2 bushels, so that excess demand is negative.

9. I now turn to the more serious case where some agent's indifference curves are actually concave (or, by extension, have concave parts). This case is illustrated in Figure 7E, where the agent's indifference curves are quarter circles, and his endowment is α. When the budget line is that through β his demand is again not uniquely defined: it may be α or β, but not now any bundle between these. More importantly, where this is uniquely defined his demand does not change continuously as price changes. If the price is below that represented by the budget line through β his demand will definitely be α, while if the price is slightly above this level his demand will be a bundle near to β. Thus his demand for wheat jumps from the positive quantity contained in his endowment, at α, to zero, at β, at this price.

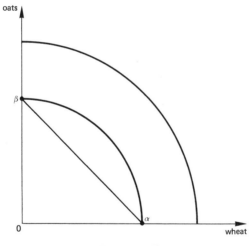

FIGURE 7E

This means that aggregate, and thus excess, demand will not be continuous, so that the excess demand curve will have a jump at this price, as illustrated in Figure 7F. If the jump occurs as illustrated then the excess demand curve will no longer intersect the horizontal axis, and there will be no equilibrium price. At the price where the jump occurs excess demand may be positive or negative but cannot be zero, while at any other price excess demand is either definitely positive or definitely negative. This illustrated in the following example.

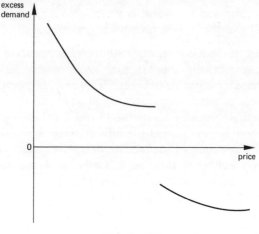

FIGURE 7F

10. *Example 7C*. The economy is that of Example 3C (3.15) except that Leon has concave preferences defined by assigning the utility level $x^2 + y^2$ instead of xy; his indifference curves are thus the quarter circles illustrated in Figure 7E. When $p = 1$ Karl's demand for wheat is 1 bushel, as in Example 3B (3.12), but Leon's is not uniquely defined: it may be zero or 2 bushels, that is at β or α respectively in Figure 7E. If in fact Leon's demand is zero then excess demand is negative, while if his demand is 2 bushels then excess demand is positive. Thus this price is not an equilibrium.

If p is less than 1 then Leon's demand for wheat is 2 bushels and Karl's is positive, so that excess demand is positive. If p is greater than 1 then Leon's demand for wheat is zero and Karl's is less than 2 bushels, so that excess demand is negative. It follows that at no price can excess demand be zero, so that there can be no equilibrium.

11. The problem of the possible non-existence of equilibrium if preferences are not convex does not arise in large economies, that is economies with many agents of each type. The reason for this is that although individual demands may not continuous average demand will be, and this is sufficient for equilibrium to exist.

If an agent had the preferences illustrated in Figure 7E, and the endowment α in that figure, his demand when the budget line was that through β would be either α or β, and thus be discontinuous at the implied price, as seen in Section 7.9. Now if there were two agents of this type each might choose α, each might choose β, or one might choose α and the other β. Average demand would then be either α, or β, or the mid-point of α and β. In the same way if there were n agents of this type average demand would be either α, or β, or any of the $n-1$ equally spaced bundles between α and β. As the number of agents of this type becomes infinite average demand becomes either α, or β, or any bundle between these, so that the mean excess demand curve no longer has a jump at this price, but instead has a vertical segment, as seen in Section 7.7.

This is illustrated for a finite number of agents in Figure 7G, the excess demand curve of which becomes that of Figure 7D as the number of agents becomes infinite. Thus, just as in the case of linear preferences, there will always be a potential equilibrium even if preferences are non-convex, provided there are sufficiently many agents of each type.

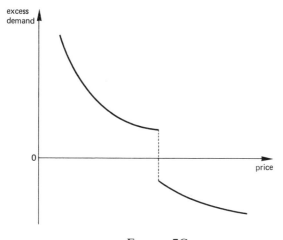

FIGURE 7G

12. Not only will there always be an exact potential equilibrium if there are infinitely many agents of each type, but there will also be an approximate potential equilibrium if there is a large but finite number of such agents. By there being an approximate potential equilibrium I mean that if I specify any positive amount, however small, there will be some number of agents of each type for, and beyond, which mean excess demand may be smaller than this amount. This follows directly from the argument of Section 7.11, illustrated in Figure 7G, where the

isolated points in the vertical segment of the excess demand curve may be made arbitratrily close to each other, and thus one of these arbitrarily close to the horizontal axis, by increasing the number of agents.

The interpretation of an approximate potential equilibrium is that of a price at which all agents can make nearly all their planned exchanges, or equivalently, as a price at which nearly all agents can make all their planned exchanges.

13. In the discussions of coalitions and manipulation in large economies the balance in the numbers of agents of each type played a critical role. This is not the case here, where there may be completely different numbers of agents of different types, provided there are sufficiently many of each type that has non-convex preferences. This is because average demand by each type is continuous if there are sufficiently many agents of this type, irrespective of how many agents there may be of other types. Indeed, since average demand by any type with convex preferences is continuous anyway there may be any numbers, large or small, of agents of such types.

8 Continuity

1. Given that equilibrium prices exist I now enquire whether such prices depend continuously on the attributes of the economy. This will be the case if equilibrium prices change only slowly as the preferences and endowments of the agents change; if this were not the case then the theory of value would have little empirical relevance. To return to the analogy of the ball and the spring, the theory of weight would be unsatisfactory if an arbitrarily small change in the diameter of the ball lead to a large change in the length of the spring, for then an approximate knowledge of the diameter of the ball, which is all that is available in practice, would not determine the weight of the ball even approximately.

To answer this question I first examine the relation between the excess demands of an economy and its attributes, and the continuity of this relation. I then use this to explore the relation between equilibrium prices and attributes, and note that discontinuities may occur in special cases. Finally, I explain what is meant by almost all economies, and show that continuity applies in almost all economies.

The answer to this question is quite satisfactory. In almost all economies equilibrium prices depend continuously on the attributes of the economy.

2. To investigate the relationship between the attributes of an economy and its equilibrium prices I shall start by investigating that between the attributes of the economy and its excess demand curve. As was noted in Section 7.3, we may associate an excess demand curve with any economy, or collection of attributes. I now show that the converse is also true, that is that we can find some economy, or collection of attributes, which generates any given excess demand curve over any range of regular prices, provided of course that this curve is continuous.

To do this I first construct an economy in which excess demand is zero at all regular prices. In this economy Leon is endowed with 2 bushels of wheat only, and Karl with 2 bushels of oats only. Leon's preferences are smooth and scale-independent, and defined by specifying the rate of substitution on a ray to be the slope of the line from the endowment allocation α to the point δ where the ray intersects the line joining the allocation β, in which Leon has 1 bushel of wheat only, to the allocation γ, in which Karl has 1 bushel of oats only; this is illustrated in Figure 8A. Karl's preferences are defined similarly, his rate of substitution on his ray through δ being the slope of the line from α to δ.

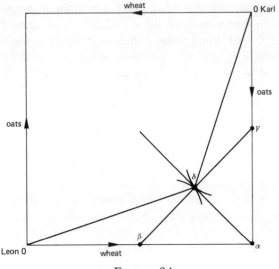

FIGURE 8A

Note that this specification does not define Leon's rate of substitution on rays above his ray through γ, nor Karl's on those above his through β; rates of substitution on such rays may be taken as infinite, as they are on the rays through γ and β respectively. This means that these preferences do not have the properties assumed in Section 3.4 at all bundles, but they do have these properties at all bundles which the relevant agent would demand at any regular price, which is sufficient for our purposes. It is because preferences do not have the required properties everywhere that excess demand can be zero at all positive prices but still be infinite when price is zero, that is be discontinuous at zero price.

At any allocation such as δ on the line from β to γ each agent has the same rate of substitution, namely the slope of the line from the endowment allocation, α, to δ. This means that if the line from α

through δ is a budget line then each agent will plan δ, so that δ is an equilibrium allocation and the slope of this line is an equilibrium price. Since this applies to any such δ between β and γ, and thus to any regularly sloped budget line, it follows that all regular prices are equilibrium prices, or that excess demand is zero at all such prices.

Using this economy as a point of departure I now construct an economy with any given small (continuous) excess demand curve, that is where the given excess demand is sufficiently small at all regular prices. To do this note that we may alternatively define Leon's preferences in exactly the same way as above, but replacing the line from β to γ in this definition with any continuous curve sufficiently close to this line, as illustrated in Figure 8B. If Karl has the same preferences as above, that is those determined by the line rather than the curve, then at any given price Leon's demand will be the point ε where the budget line intersects the curve while Karl's will be at the point δ where the budget line intersects the line. The excess demand for wheat at this price will therefore be the horizontal distance from δ to ε, being positive if ε is to the east of δ and negative if it is to the west.

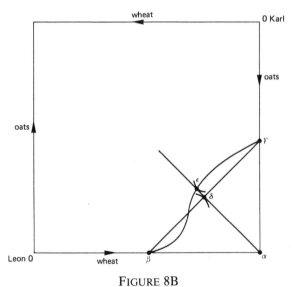

FIGURE 8B

This means that we may construct the required economy by specifying the curve defining Leon's preferences to be such that the horizontal distance between the point where this curve intersects the budget line at any regular price and that where the line defining Karl's preferences intersects this budget line is equal to the required excess demand at this price.

Finally, using this intermediary economy I construct an economy with any given continuous excess demand curve, not necessarily small. To do this note that each agent's preferences in the intermediary economy are smooth and scale-independent. Now if an agent has smooth scale-independent preferences then the price ratio is the same as the agent's rate of substitution, and this rate of substitution depends only on the ratio in which he demands wheat and oats. This means that the ratio in which he demands wheat and oats depends only on the price ratio, and not on his endowment, so that if his endowment doubles, say, then so does his demand for each commodity. This is illustrated in Figure 8C.

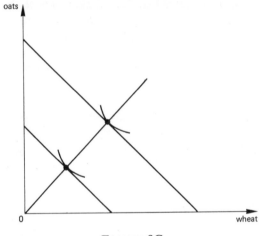

FIGURE 8C

It follows that doubling each agent's endowment doubles aggregate demand as well as aggregate supply, and thus doubles excess demand. In the light of this we may construct an economy with any given continuous excess demand curve by first constructing the intermediary economy with the small excess demand curve where excess demand at any price is a fraction $1/h$ of that required, this fraction being as small as necessary, and then multiplying each agent's endowment in this intermediary economy by the factor h.

We may thus construct an economy which generates any given excess demand curve. However, while there is only one excess demand curve we may associate with any given economy there will be many economies which generate any given excess demand curve. For example, if we give Leon's attributes to Karl and conversely then we have a different economy, but of course the same excess demand curve.

3. Similar economies have similar excess demand curves, in that a small change in any agent's preferences or endowment results in only a small change in excess demand at any price. This is because a small change in an agent's preferences or his endowment has a small effect on his demand, as noted in Section 3.11, and thus a small effect on aggregate demand, and either no effect, if preferences vary, or a small effect, if endowments vary, on aggregate supply, and therefore a small effect on excess demand at any given price.

4. We cannot expect the converse of this to be true, that is for similar excess demand curves to be generated only by similar economies. Indeed, as we have seen, even some given excess demand curve may be generated by two substantially different economies. However, similar excess demand curves can be generated by similar economies, that is there is always some economy similar to any given economy which has any specified excess demand curve similar to that of the given economy.

The reason for this is that we may obtain any given small change in an agent's demand by making some suitable small change to his preferences, as is illustrated in Figure 8D. By doing this we may obtain any required small change in the agent's demand at all regular prices, and thus in aggregate and excess demand at all such prices. Strictly speaking, this only applies if the agent's original demand for each commodity is positive. However, at and, because of continuity of demands, near any equilibrium price some agent must have a positive demand for wheat and some agent a positive demand for oats, so by choosing the appropriate agent we may still to this at all prices at and near an equilibrium, which is sufficient for our purposes.

5. Having explored the relation between the economy and its excess demand curve I now turn to that between the economy and its equilibrium prices, and the continuity of this relation.

I shall first consider the case where the excess demand curve of the given economy is not flat, that is its slope is not zero, at any equilibrium price. Note that this requires the slope to be defined, that is the excess demand curve to be smooth, and I shall therefore assume this to be the case in this and the following section; this involves no serious

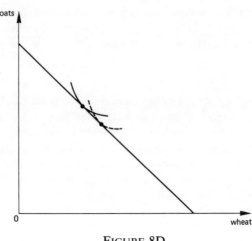

FIGURE 8D

restriction as we may always construct a smooth excess demand curve
as close as we choose to any (continuous) excess demand curve which
is not smooth. In this case, where the given excess demand curve is not
flat at any equilibrium, the excess demand curve of any sufficiently
similar economy, which will be close to the excess demand curve of the
given economy, will intersect the horizontal axis only at prices close to
those where the excess demand curve of the given economy intersects
this axis. This is illustrated in Figure 8E, where the solid   excess
demand curve is that of the given economy and the broken curves
those of two similar economies. Thus in this case a small change in
attributes leads to only a small change in equilibrium prices.

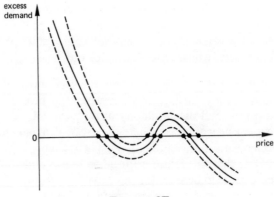

FIGURE 8E

However, if the excess demand curve of the original economy is flat at some equilibrium, in which case the economy is said to be critical, a small change in attributes may lead to a large change in equilibrium prices. In Figure 8F the given economy, whose excess demand curve is the solid one, has two equilibria, but an arbitrarily similar economy, whose excess demand curve is the broken one, has only one. Although the second economy is similar to the first it has no equilibrium price similar to the lower equilibrium price of the first economy, although it does have one similar to the higher.

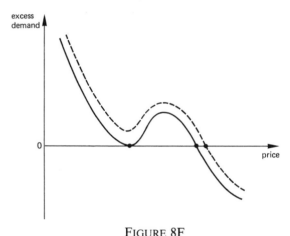

FIGURE 8F

Note that even if the given economy is critical an arbitrary small change in its attributes may still lead to only a small change in equilibrium; this is illustrated in Figure 8G, where the solid excess demand curve (which momentarily becomes flat at the point where it crosses the horizontal axis) is that of a critical economy and the broken one that of an economy similar to this.

We may conclude that equilibrium prices depend continuously on the attributes of the economy provided the economy is not critical, but may or may not do so in critical economies. This conclusion is only satisfactory if critical economies are rare in some sense, that is if almost all economies are non-critical (sometimes known as regular). I shall now show that this is the case.

6. There are infinitely many possible economies, and there may therefore be infinitely many possible critical economies. In the light of this I propose the following interpretation: almost all economies are

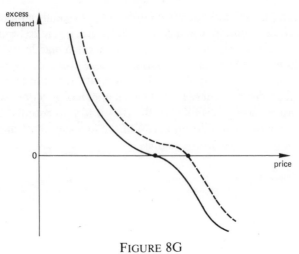

FIGURE 8G

non-critical if there is some non-critical economy close to any critical economy, but not conversely, that is if all economies sufficiently close to a non-critical economy are non-critical.

This interpretation may be illustrated by means of analogy. Consider all fractions between 0 and 1, and define all those that are (integral) powers of 1/2, that is 1/2, 1/4, 1/8 and so forth, to be critical. Then there is some non-critical fraction close to any critical one: for example, the fraction $1/8 + 1/h$ is non-critical if h is larger than 8, and may be made as close as required to the critical fraction 1/8 by making h sufficiently large. Also, all fractions sufficiently close to a non-critical fraction are non-critical: for example, all fractions differing by less than 1/12 from the non-critical fraction 1/3 are non-critical. It follows that almost all fractions are non-critical. This formalises the idea that although there are infinitely many critical fractions there are infinitely more non-critical ones, or that almost all fractions are non-critical.

Given this interpretation I now show that almost all economies are non-critical. Firstly, there is always some non-critical economy close to a critical one. This is because we may always obtain the excess demand curve of a non-critical economy by making a small change to the excess demand curve of a critical one, as is illustrated in Figure 8F, and this non-critical economy may be chosen so as to be similar to the given critical economy, as noted in Section 8.4. Secondly, all economies sufficiently close to a non-critical economy are non-critical. This is because a small change in attributes leads to only a small change in the excess demand curve, and if there is a small change in the excess demand curve of a non-critical economy the resulting excess demand curve is also that of a non-critical economy, as is illustrated in Figure 8E.

9 Uniqueness

1. Given that equilibrium prices exist and depend continuously on attributes I now enquire whether such prices are unique. This will be the case if there is only one price at which the plans of all the agents are compatible; if this were not the case, and particularly if there were infinitely many equilibrium prices, then the theory of value would be ambiguous. To return to the analogy of the ball and spring, the theory of weight would be unsatisfactory if the force of gravity balanced that of the spring at more than one length, for then a given ball would have more than one weight.

To answer this question I first show that in almost all economies the number of equilibria is finite, but equilibrium may not be unique. I then explain the concept of a representative economy and the sense in which economies are likely to be representative, and show that in such economies equilibrium is unique. Finally, I extend the discussion to economies with multiple markets and confirm that equilibrium is unique in representative economies, but may also be unique in other economies.

The answer to this question is not unsatisfactory. The number of equilibria is almost always finite, and equilibrium is likely to be unique.

2 . I shall first show that although an economy may have infinitely many equilibria, as is illustrated in Figure 9A, it cannot have infinitely many separated equilibria. Because the excess demand for wheat is continuous and always positive at low prices it can only be zero at a finite number of separated prices p (of wheat in terms of oats) less than 1. Similarly, the excess demand for oats can only be zero at a finite number of separated values of $1/p$, the price of oats in terms of wheat, less than 1, that is values of p greater than 1. Because of Walras' law the excess demand for wheat can only be zero if the excess demand for oats is zero, so there can only be a finite number of separate values of p at which the excess demand for wheat is zero, that is equilibrium values.

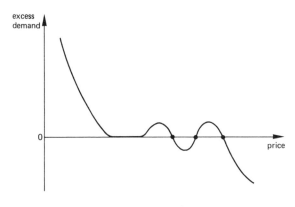

FIGURE 9A

Clearly there can only be adjacent equilibria if the excess demand curve is flat at these equilibria, as in Figure 9A, that is in critical economies. Since almost all economies are non-critical, as was noted in Section 8.6, it follows that in almost all economies the number of equilibria is finite, which is to say that any equilibrium is locally unique in that it is the only equilibrium in some range. (As in Section 8.5, it is assumed in this section that all excess demand curves are smooth.) Note that even if the economy is critical the number of equilibria may still be finite, and indeed equilibrium may be unique: for example, equilibrium is unique in the critical economy where continuity applied discussed in Section 8.5.

If the excess demand curve is never flat at equilibrium it must interesect the horizontal axis wherever it meets it, and cannot be tangential. Because the excess demand curve is above the axis at low prices and below the axis at high prices this means that in such economies the excess demand curve must interesect the horizontal axis an odd number of times. It follows that in almost all economies not only is the number of equilibria finite, but also that it is odd. There is, however, no supposition that equilibrium is unique: for example, if the excess demand of the economy of Figure 9A is increased slightly at all prices then the economy becomes non-critical but there are still three equilibria.

3. To examine when equilibrium is unique, rather than equilibria being only finite in number, I shall start by considering a non-critical economy in which all agents have the same preferences and endowments. At any equilibrium price p their common demands must be the

same as their common endowments, say α, and at any disequilibrium price their common demands must be some different bundle, say β. This is illustrated in Figure 9B, which shows that β must lie outside the budget line for the equilibrium price p. This means that the value at p of the bundle β must be greater than that of α, which is to say that the value at p of the excess demand, that is the difference between β and α, is positive.

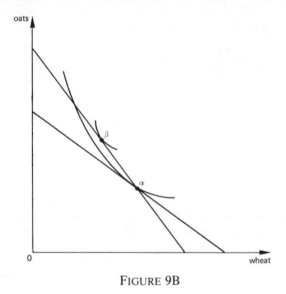

FIGURE 9B

If all agents are similar then this property will continue to apply, since a small change in preferences or endowments leads to only a small change in excess demands, as noted in Section 8.3. Indeed, to quote Wald (page 375), who first considered this property: if the property does not apply 'then there must be special relationship between the demands of the individuals, which are statistically improbable'. With this in mind I shall refer to a non-critical economy in which this property, of the value at any equilibrium price of the excess demand expressed at any disequilibrium price always being positive, applies as a representative economy. (Sometimes any economy with this property is known as a revealed preference economy.) Following Wald, I shall consider it 'likely' that an economy is representative, though clearly this concept is subjective, and much weaker than that of 'almost all' economies being non-critical. (The likelihood of an economy being representative is returned to in Section 9.4.)

The essential reason why a non-critical economy in which all agents are the same is representative is that each agent's demand is the same as his endowment, that is that no exchanges are made at the equilibrium price. It follows that if this property of no exchanges being made at the equilibrium price applies in a non-critical economy for whatever reason, or even if all exchanges at the equilibrium price are small, then the economy is representative. Note that this shows that an economy may be representative even though its agents have markedly different preferences and endowments.

4. I now show that equilibrium must be unique in a representative economy. Assume that there is more than one equilibrium price, and choose any two, say p and q; then the average, or mid-point, of these two prices, say r, must also be an equilibrium. If it were not then the value at the equilibrium price p of the excess demand expressed at the disequilibrium price r would be positive, as would the value at q of this excess demand, because the economy is representative. This would mean that the average of these two values, that is the value at r of the excess demand expressed at r, would be positive, which would contradict Walras' law, which says that this value is zero. Thus r must also be an equilibrium price. A similar argument shows that all prices between p and q must be equilibria, so that there are infinitely many equilibria. This is impossible in a non-critical economy, which means that the initial assumption that there was more than one equilibrium price must be false.

Note that even if all agents have the same preferences and endowments equilibrium may not be unique if the economy is critical. This is illustrated in Figure 9C, where preferences are not smooth. At each of the prices shown the common demands are the same as the common endowment, α, so that both prices are equilibria. Indeed, any price between these two is also an equilibrium. Of course this cannot happen if preferences are smooth, for then the rate of substitution at α would be well-defined and equal to the slope of the budget line, so there could be only one appropriate budget line and thus only one equilibrium price.

Restricting our attention to non-critical economies, if p is an equilibrium price and x and y bushels are the excess demands for wheat and oats respectively expressed at some other price q then the economy is representative if and only if $px + y$ is always positive. Since $qx + y$ is always zero because of Walras' law this is equivalent to dx always being negative, where $d = q - p$ is the (nonzero) difference between the price q at which the excess demand x is expressed and the

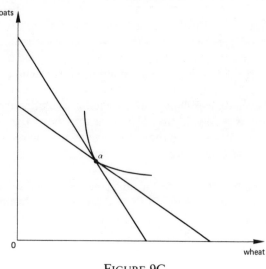

FIGURE 9C

equilibrium price p. This in turn is equivalent to excess demand being positive at all prices below p, where d is negative, and negative at all prices above p, where d is positive, as illustrated in Figure 9D. Now it is clear that equilibrium is unique if and only if the excess demand curve has this general shape. It follows that (in a single-market economy) not only is equilibrium unique if the economy is representative, but also that equilibrium cannot be unique unless the economy is representative. Fortunately, this is not the case in economies with more than one market, that is with more than two commodities, where although equilibrium will still be unique in representative economies it may also be unique in economies which are not representative.

An implication of this is that if a (single-market) economy is not representative then its excess demand curve must have some upward-sloping part, which is to say that the aggregate demand for wheat must rise as its price rises. Since such a response is seldom observed this argument reinforces our considering it 'likely' that an economy is representative.

5. In the light of this I shall now extend the discussion to economies with multiple markets, which I shall represent by those with three commodities, say wheat, barley and oats. Everything I have demonstrated in the context of single-market economies also applies, with the appropriate changes, in that of multiple-market economies. To

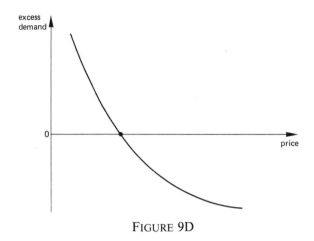

FIGURE 9D

avoid repetition I shall therefore discuss only the essentials of the framework of such economies.

I shall continue to express prices in terms of oats, but now have two such prices: that of wheat in terms of oats and that of barley in terms of oats. At any given combination of these two prices excess demands are defined for all three commodities. However, these excess demands are related by Walras' law, so that if the excess demand for any two commodities is zero then so is that for the third. A price combination is therefore an equilibrium if the resulting excess demands for both wheat and barley, say, are zero.

The economy may be illustrated in a figure known as a Hicksian cross. In this I shall assume, for simplicity, that the economy is such that if the excess demand for wheat is zero at some price combination then a small change in the price of wheat, leaving the price of barley unchanged, will make this excess demand either positive or negative, and similarly for barley and oats; this involves no serious restriction as we may always obtain this property if necessary by making arbitrary small changes to excess demands.

All possible price combinations are illustrated in Figure 9E, where the horizontal distance from the origin to some point such as λ represents the price of wheat in terms of oats at the price combination λ, and the vertical distance the price of barley in terms of oats. (Note that this is a new interpretation of such L-shaped figures; this new interpretation applies to all such figures henceforth.)

Take any price of barley and note the price of wheat at which the resulting excess demand for wheat is zero. There will be some such

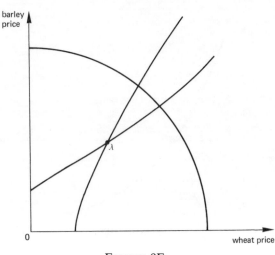

FIGURE 9E

price because excess demand is positive at low prices and negative at high.There may by more than one such price but these must be separated, because of the simplifying assumption made above. By doing this for all possible prices of barley we may obtain the locus of price combinations at which the excess demand for wheat is zero; this is illustrated by the curve which meets only the horizontal axis in Figure 9E. This locus is continuous because excess demand is continuous, and it keeps away from the vertical axis because excess demand is positive at sufficiently low prices. Apart from these restrictions the locus may have any shape, since continuous excess demand curves may have any shape (at regular prices), as noted in Section 8.2.

In the same way we may obtain the locus of price combinations at which the excess demand for barley is zero. This has the same properties as the locus for wheat; it is illustrated by the curve which meets only the vertical axis in Figure 9E. A price combination such as λ where these two loci intersect is one where the excess demands for both wheat and barley are zero, and thus an equilibrium.

6. It is worthwhile confirming directly that there will always be an equilibrium, and that this will be unique if the economy is representative.

At all price combinations sufficiently close to the origin both prices are small, so that both excess demands must be positive. Now consider excess demands at price combinations some sufficiently large given distance from the origin, that is on the circumference of a large circle centred on the origin, as illustrated in Figure 9E. At any such combination the price of either wheat or barley in terms of oats is large, which is to say that the price of oats in terms of either wheat or barley is small, so that the excess demand for oats is positive. Then because of Walras' law the excess demand for either wheat or barley must be negative. Given the properties of the loci the only way in which both excess demands can be positive at all combinations near the origin and at least one excess demand negative at all combinations some given large distance from the origin is for the loci to cross. It follows that equilibrium always exists.

We may confirm that equilibrium is unique if the economy is representative by using the same argument as in Section 9.4. If λ and μ, say, are both equilibrium combinations then so is their average, or mid-point, say v. If it were not then the value at the equilibrium combination λ of the excess demands expressed at the disequilibrium combination v would be positive, as would the value at μ of these excess demands. This would mean that the average of these values, that is the value at v of the excess demands expressed at v, would be positive, which would contradict Walras' law. Thus v must also be an equilibrium combination. A similar argument shows that all combinations between λ and μ must be equilibria, which is impossible in a non-critical economy. It follows that equilibrium is unique.

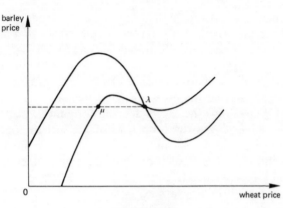

barley
price

0

wheat price

FIGURE 9F

7. With this background I now show that equilibrium may be unique even if the economy is not representative, as claimed in Section 9.4. This is illustrated in Figure 9F, where equilibrium is unique, at λ. Assume that this economy is representative. Then just as in Section 9.4, if the excess demands for wheat and barley are x and y bushels when their prices differ from their equilibrium values by d and e respectively, not both zero, $dx + ey$ must be negative. This means that if the price of barley is kept at its equilibrium level, that is if e is zero, then x cannot be zero unless d is zero. This in turn means that, given that the price of barley is at its equilibrium level there is no price of wheat, other than its equilibrium price, at which the excess demand for wheat is zero. Clearly this is not the case in Figure 9F, where the excess demand for wheat is also zero at the combination μ. It follows that the economy is not representative.

10 Stability

1. Given that equilibrium prices exist, depend continuously on attributes, and are likely to be unique I now enquire whether such prices are stable. This will be the case if prices converge to their equilibrium levels; if this were not the case then the theory of value would have little practical relevance. To return to the analogy of the ball and spring, the theory of weight would be unsatisfactory if there were no forces, such as friction, to bring the spring to its equilibrium length, for then this equilibrium length would seldom, if ever, be observed.

To answer this question I first discuss the mechanism by which prices are adjusted, and show that given this mechanism equilibrium is stable in all representative economies. I then extend the discussion to economies with multiple markets and confirm that equilibrium is stable in representative economies, but may be stable or unstable in other economies.

The answer to this question is not unsatisfactory. Equilibrium prices are likely to be stable, and are definitely so in the class of economies where uniqueness is ensured.

2. To discuss stability, which is a dynamic concept, I must first discuss the mechanism which determines how prices move. Since each agent takes prices as given no agent can change prices directly. This means that any specification of how prices move must be arbitrary, in the sense that it is not determined by the preferences and endowments of the agents.

The mechanism I assume (which is sometimes known as the tatonnement mechanism) changes prices in proportion to excess demands. Thus if demand is too high, that is if excess demand is positive, then price rises, and the larger the excess demand the larger the price rise. Similarly, if demand is too low then price falls. Of course if demand is neither too high nor too low, that is if excess demand is zero, then price does not change. In this process the interval between price changes is taken to be very small, so that adjustment is almost continuous over time. Note that price can never become zero, or negative, under this process because once price becomes sufficiently near to zero excess demand becomes positive, so that price rises.

There are two conceptual problems with this adjustment mechanism which require comment. The first is that it requires some outside agent, or auctioneer, to change prices. As noted, this is inevitable if no agent in the economy can influence prices.

The second is that it requires there to be no actual exchanges of commodities at any disequilibrium price, but only the making of provisional plans by each agent, plans which are consummated only if they are all possible, that is if the price is an equilibrium. This is inevitable if we are to investigate the stability of some given economy, that is collection of preferences and endowments. If some exchanges are made at a disequilibrium price then the endowments of the agents, and thus the specification of the economy, changes. This means that the eventual equilibrium may depend on the arbitrary initial equilibrium price at which these are made, and the rationing process that determines which exchanges are actually made, as well as on the initial attributes of the economy. Of course exchanges at an equilibrium price also change the specification of the economy, but the equilibrium of the after-exchange economy will be the same as the equilibrium of the original economy, at which these exchanges were made; indeed, this is one meaning of the concept of equilibrium. (This question of possible exchanges at diseqilibrium prices is returned to in Section 10.8.)

Given the adjustment mechanism I consider an equilibrium to be stable if, after starting from any initial level, price eventually converges to that equilibrium. By this I mean, more precisely, that given any positive distance, however small, after sufficient time price always remains within that distance of the equilibrium.

If the economy has multiple equilibria then no equilibrium can be stable: if price starts at one equilibrium it will of course remain there, and thus not converge to any other equilibrium. Accordingly, I only consider economies in which equilibrium is unique, in which case I shall, by extension, speak of the stability of the economy. (If there are multiple equilibria it may be that some equilibrium is stable in a weaker sense; I take up this question in Section 10.7.)

3 .A stable equilibrium (in a single-market economy) is illustrated in Figure 10A. If price is below the unique equilibrium then excess demand is positive so that price increases, as shown by the arrow,

while if price is above the equilibrium then excess demand is negative and price falls, also as shown. Since the change at any stage of the process is small, the distance between the price at any stage and the equilibrium price is always decreasing, so that the price converges to equilibrium.

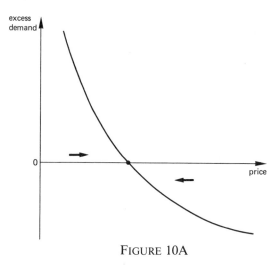

FIGURE 10A

This makes it clear that a representative economy is stable. As noted in Section 9.4, in a representative economy equilibrium is unique, and excess demand is always positive at any price below equilibrium and negative at any price above equilibrium. Thus the excess demand curve of such an economy has the general shape of that illustrated in Figure 10A, and the economy is stable.

A more precise argument is as follows. The unique equilibrium, say p, of a representative economy is stable if the distance between the price at any stage of the adjustment process, say q, and this equilibrium price is always decreasing, or equivalently if the square of this distance is always decreasing. If the excess demand expressed at the price q is x bushels then the price adjustment at q is ax, where a is the arbitrary change of price per bushel of excess demand at each adjustment. The relevant squared distance before the price adjustment is d^2, where d is the price difference $q - p$, while that after the adjustment is $(d + ax)^2$, so that the difference between these is $a^2x^2 + 2adx$. The squared distance is decreasing if this difference is negative, that is, as a is positive, if dx is less than $-\frac{1}{2}ax^2$. Since adjustment is almost continuous the constant a can be taken as being arbitrarily small, by making the interval between price changes arbitrarily small. This means that the squared distance will be decreasing if dx is negative; but as noted in Section 9.4, this is always the case in a representative economy.

It follows immediately from this, and the argument of Section 9.3, that any non-critical economy in which all agents are similar, or for any other reason make only small exchanges at equilibrium, is stable. An application of this is as follows. Consider any economy, and assume that somehow, perhaps by chance, an equilibrium is reached, at which exchanges are made. Then the new economy formed by these exchanges of endowments will have the same equilibrium price as the original economy, though of course no new exchanges will be made at this price. It follows that the new economy will (almost always) be representative, and therefore stable. Thus if the endowments of an economy are not given arbitrarily, but are the result of some previous equilibrium exchanges, then the economy will (almost always) be stable.

Restricting our attention to non-critical economies, it was noted in Section 9.4 that a (single-market) economy with a unique equilibrium must be representative. This means that a unique equilibrium must automatically be stable. Further, not only is a representative economy stable, but also an economy cannot be stable unless it is representative, since if it were not representative it would have multiple equilibria. This is not the case in multiple-market economies, to which I now return.

4. When two prices adjust there are two arbitrary constants to consider: the change of price per bushel of excess demand for wheat, and that for barley. To keep the exposition simple I shall choose the units of measurement of these two commodities so that these two constants are the same. For example, the constant for barley is measured in terms of bushels of oats per bushel of barley (that is price) per bushel of barley (that is excess demand), so if this is four times the constant for wheat when barley is measured in bushels it will be the same as that for wheat if barley is measured in 'double-bushels'.

With multiple markets an economy may be unstable even though equilibrium is unique. This is illustrated in Figure 10B, where equilibrium is unique; note that the argument used in Section 9.7 shows that the economy is not representative.

Because the excess demand for wheat is positive near the origin it will be positive at all price combinations to the north of the locus for

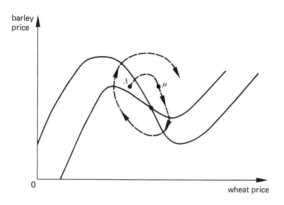

FIGURE 10B

wheat, and negative at all combinations to the south of this. Similarly, the excess demand for barley will be positive at all combinations to the south of the locus for barley, and negative at all combinations to the north of this. Thus at a combination such as λ both excess demands will be positive, so that both prices will rise, as shown. On the other hand, at a combination such as μ the excess demand for wheat will be positive, so that the price of wheat will rise but that for barley will be negative, so that its price will fall, also as shown. Price movements in the other sectors, which are in the directions of the arrows shown in these, are obtained in the same way. These arrows make it clear that price moves around its equilibrium level in a spiral, illustrated by the broken curve in the figure. This spiral may be converging, in which case the economy will be stable, or it may be diverging, as shown, in which case it will be unstable.

5. We may confirm that a representative multiple-market economy is stable using the same argument as in Section 10.3. If the excess demands for wheat and barley are x and y bushels when their prices differ from their unique equilibrium values by d and e respectively then $dx + ey$ must be negative, as noted in Section 9.7. The squared distance between this price combination and the equilibrium combination is now $d^2 + e^2$, and, using the same argument as in Section 10.3, this is decreasing if, and only if, $dx + ey$ is less than $-\frac{1}{2}a(x^2 + y^2)$, where a is the common adjustment constant. Since a can be taken as arbitrarily small this will always be the case if and only if $dx + ey$ is negative, that is if and only if the economy is representative. Thus a representative economy is stable.

6. This argument also makes it clear that the distance between the price combination at any stage of the adjustment process and the equilibrium combination will always be decreasing only if the economy is representative. However, this does not mean that the economy cannot be stable unless it is representative. Provided that equilibrium is unique, this distance can be increasing at some combinations and decreasing at others, and the economy still be stable.

An economy which is stable but not representative is illustrated in Figure 10C, where equilibrium is unique. In this figure the circumference of the circle centred on the equilibrium is the set of all combinations some given distance from the equilibrium; the arrows on this circle show the direction of price changes at such combinations, obtained in the same way as in Section 10.4.

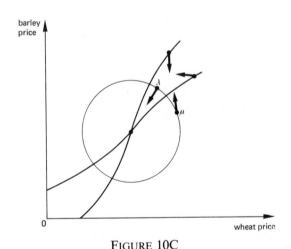

FIGURE 10C

At a combination such as λ the distance from equilibrium is definitely decreasing, as both prices fall and movement is to the inside of the circle, as shown. Further, once the price combination is inside or on the boundary of the sector containing λ it will always remain in that sector, since all movement is inwards, also as shown. However, at a combination such as μ the price of wheat falls and that of barley rises, so that movement may be outwards or inwards. If movement is outwards, as shown, the distance from equilibrium is increasing so the economy cannot be representative. However, the price combination will still converge to equilibrium because the price combination must eventually enter the sector containing λ. Once in this sector it will move steadily to equilibrium, as seen. A similar argument applies to the other two sectors, so that the economy is stable. (Movement at a combination such as μ might equally well have been inward, in which case the relevant distance would always be decreasing, and Figure 10C would portray a representative economy.)

Note that this provides a further example of an economy which has a unique equilibrium but which is not representative. Also note that the argument used shows that if both loci are upward-sloping everywhere and equilibrium is unique then the economy must be stable.

7. It was noted in Section 10.2 that if an economy has multiple equilibria then no equilibrium can be stable, in that price converges to it after starting from any initial level. However, it may be that some equilibrium is stable in a weaker sense, that is locally stable, in that price converges to it after starting from any initial level sufficiently close to it. This only requires equilibrium to be locally unique. Local stability would be relevant if, for example, there were some small change in the preferences or endowments of an economy which was at equilibrium. In this case the initial level would be the equilibrium of the original economy, and this would (almost always) be close to the equilibrium of the new economy, as seen in Section 8.5. Thus price would converge to its equilibrium even if this equilibrium were only locally stable.

An economy with an equilibrium which is only locally stable is illustrated in Figure 10D, where the arrows showing the direction of price changes are obtained in the same way as in Section 10.4. Prices converge to the equilibrium λ after starting from any initial combination in the quadrant below the combination μ; this may be seen by using the argument of Section 10.6. It follows that the equilibrium λ is locally stable, but only locally so as equilibrium is not unique. Indeed, for the same reasons, prices converge to the equilibrium v after starting from any initial combination in the quadrant above μ, so that v is also locally stable. However, the equilibrium μ is not even locally stable since prices definitely diverge from μ after starting from any initial combination in the quadrant below μ, or in that above μ, however close to μ this initial combination may be. Thus prices may converge to some equilibrium in practice even though this equilibrium is not unique, and thus not fully stable.

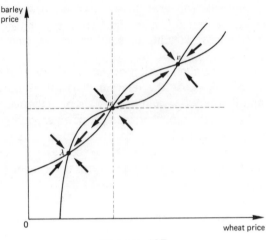

FIGURE 10D

8. Finally, I shall consider the effect of permitting exchanges to be made at disequilibrium prices, that is allowing the endowments, and thus the economy, to change at the same time as prices are changing.

A problem which now arises is that the actual exchanges made at disequilibrium prices are arbitrary: if there are excess demands then some planned exchanges cannot be made, but we do not know which. However, we may reasonably assume that if any exchanges are made then some agent is better off and no agent worse off as a result, and that if some agent can be made better off and no agent worse off by making exchanges then some exchanges will be made. Note that, although apparently reasonable, this assumption does not permit an agent to speculate, that is, say, to acquire wheat which he does not want in the expectation of later being able to exchange this for oats at a more advantageous price.

Now as exchanges are always made at any allocation which is not an optimum, and as such exchanges make some agents better off and none worse off, endowments must converge to some optimum allocation. The price at this stage may not be an equilibrium price for the economy with this endowment allocation, but if it is not then price will continue to change according to excess demands, while endowments remain fixed. As no exchanges are made at any of these prices no exchanges will be made at the equilibrium price, so that, as noted in Section 10.3, this equilibrium will (almost always) be stable.

Since this argument applies whatever the characteristics of the given economy, that is whether it is representative or not, permitting dis-equilibrium exchanges tends to increase stability. However, as endowments, and thus the economy, change as a result of such exchanges this tells us nothing about the stability of the equilibrium of the original economy.

11 Prediction

1. Given that equilibrium prices exist, depend continuously on attributes, and are likely to be unique and stable I now enquire whether such prices depend in a predictable way on the attributes of the economy. This will be the case if the equilibrium price of a commodity rises when the commodity becomes scarcer; if this were not the case then the theory of value would have little predictive power. To return to the analogy of the ball and spring, the theory of weight would be unsatisfactory if the spring sometimes shortened when the diameter of the ball was increased, particularly if it also sometimes lengthened, for then changes in weight could not be predicted on the basis of changes in diameter.

To answer this question I first explain what is meant by a commodity becoming scarcer, and show that equilibrium prices increase when commodities become scarcer in this sense in representative economies. I then extend the discussion to economies with multiple markets and confirm that equilibrium is predictable in representative economies, but may or may not be so in other economies. Finally, I consider the case where all commodities are substitutes for each other, and show that in this case more detailed predictions may be obtained.

The answer to this question is not unsatisfactory. Equilibrium prices are likely to depend in a predictable way on the attributes of the economy, and definitely do so in the class of economies where uniqueness is ensured. If assumptions about substitutability between commodities are made then quite detailed predictions may be obtained.

2. I start by specifying what is meant by a commodity becoming scarcer. I shall consider the economy to be defined by its excess demand curve rather than by its underlying preferences and endowments, so that this specification will be in terms of this excess demand curve. I consider wheat to become scarcer, relative to oats, if there is a shift in demand from oats to wheat so that the excess demand for wheat is raised at all prices; because of Walras' law this shift in excess

demand must lower the excess demand for oats correspondingly. This specification is quite general, and allows the shift to be due to a change in preferences or in endowments.

After such a shift in demand we have a new excess demand curve, and thus new equilibrium prices. My object is to compare these new equilibria with the original equilibria, and, particularly, to determine whether the price of wheat in terms of oats definitely increases when wheat becomes scarcer relative to oats. If this is the case then I consider the economy to be predictable. (Of course the economy could also be considered to be predictable if the price of wheat definitely decreases when wheat becomes scarcer, but, as we shall see, we need not pursue this possibility.)

If there are multiple equilibria then the direction of price changes may be ambiguous. This would be the case, for example, if the two equilibrium prices of wheat in the original economy were 1 and 4, and the two prices in the economy after the shift in excess demand were 2 and 3. Accordingly, I only consider economies in which equilibrium is unique. This restriction only applies to the original economy; as any (upward) shift in excess demand is permitted I cannot restrict the economy after the shift in this way. Note that provided equilibrium is locally unique we could investigate local prediction, that is the effect of only a small shift in excess demand, in the same way as we investigated local stability in Section 10.7; however, I do not pursue this.

3. A shift in excess demand in a representative economy is illustrated in Figure 11A, where the solid curve is the old excess demand curve and the broken curve the new one. The original excess demand curve is above the horizontal axis at all prices below the unique equilibrium and below this axis at all prices above this, as noted in Section 9.4. It is clear that all new equilibrium prices are higher than the old equilibrium price. (Thus we need not pursue the possibility of an economy being predictable in that the price of wheat definitely decreases when wheat becomes scarcer.)

A more precise argument is as follows. Assume that the unique old equilibrium price is q, the new equilibrium price (or the lowest of these if there is more than one) is p, and that the new excess demand at q is x bushels; because excess demand has increased at all prices, and was originally zero at q, x must be positive. But as shown in Section 9.4, dx must be negative in a representative economy, where $d = q - p$, so that d must be negative, which is to say that p must exceed q. It follows that

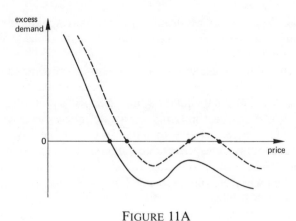

FIGURE 11A

all new equilibrium prices exceed the old equilibrium price.

Restricting our attention to non-critical economies, a (single-market) economy with a unique equilibrium must be representative, as noted in Section 9.4. This means that such an economy must automatically be predictable. Further not only is a representative economy predictable, but also an economy cannot be predictable unless it is representative, for if it were non-representative it would have multiple equilibria. This is not the case in multiple-market economies, to which I now return.

4. In economies with three commodities I continue to interpret wheat as becoming scarcer relative to oats if there is a shift in excess demand from oats to wheat which raises the excess demand for wheat at all price combinations; however, I now also specify that the excess demand for barley remain unchanged at all price combinations. In the framework of the Hicksian cross this means that after the shift the excess demand for wheat is positive at all combinations at which it was zero or positive before the shift, that is at all combinations to the west of the original locus for wheat. It follows that the new locus for wheat is to the east of the original locus. Since the excess demand for barley is unchanged at all price combinations the new locus for barley is the same as the original locus.

This is illustrated in Figure 11B, where the solid curves are the original loci and the broken curve the new locus for wheat. This shows that, with multiple markets, the economy may not be predictable even though equilibrium is unique. The old and new equilibrium combinations are λ and μ respectively, and the price of wheat is lower at μ than at λ. In this case the price of wheat has fallen when wheat has become sacrcer.

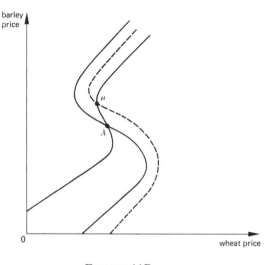

FIGURE 11B

5. We may confirm that a representative multiple-market economy is predictable using the same argument as in Section 11.3. Assume that the price of wheat at the old equilibrium exceeds that at the new equilibrium (or the new equilibrium with the lowest price of wheat if there is more than one) by an amount d, and that the price of barley at the old equilibrium exceeds that at the new by an amount e; of course d and e may be positive or negative at this stage of the argument. Then if the new excess demands for wheat and barley at the old equilibrium are x and y bushels respectively $dx + ey$ must be negative, as noted in Section 9.7. As x is positive because the excess demand for wheat has increased and y is zero because that for barley is unchanged this implies that d must be negative, which means that all new equilibrium prices of wheat exceed the old equilibrium price.

6. .An economy which is predictable but not representative is illustrated in Figure 11C. This is assumed to portray the same economy as discussed in Section 10.6, that is a non-representative economy. Nevertheless, equilibrium is unique both before and after the shift, and the price of wheat is clearly higher at the new equilibrium than at the old.

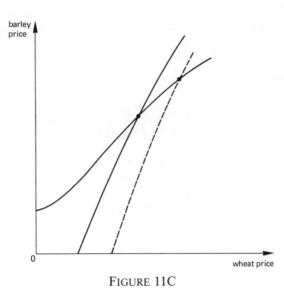

barley
price

0   wheat price

FIGURE 11C

7. While my main concern is in predicting the change in the price of the commodity which has become scarcer, here wheat, it is also of interest to consider the change in price of the commodity which is not directly affected, here barley. It is clear that even in a representative economy the price of barley may increase or decrease when wheat becomes scarcer. In Figure 11C, which, as noted in Section 10.6, may equally well portray a representative economy, the price of barley rises, while in Figure 11D, which is also (reasonably) assumed to portray a representative economy, the price of barley falls. Indeed, intuitively we should expect the price of barley to rise in response to an increase in the excess demand for wheat if barley were a substitute for wheat and to fall if it were a complement.

I shall consider what is perhaps the more typical case, at least when there are a small number of commodities, that where all commodities are substitutes for each other. The other cases, where some commodities are complementary, may be analysed using arguments similar to those employed in this case. By barley being a substitute (sometimes known to as a gross substitute) for wheat I mean that an increase in the price of wheat in terms of oats, with the price of barley in terms of oats unchanged, leads to an increase in the excess demand for barley. I shall also refer to barley as being normal if an increase in the price of barley in terms of oats, with the price of wheat in terms of oats unchanged, leads to a decrease in the excess demand for barley.

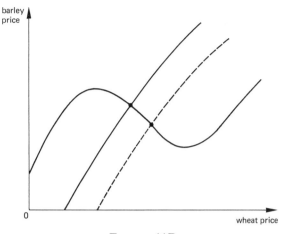

FIGURE 11D

If all commodities are substitutes for each other then they must all be normal. This is because if the price of wheat in terms of oats increases with that of barley unchanged then the excess demand for barley must increase as barley is a substitute for wheat. As the price of wheat in terms of barley has increased, with the price of oats in terms of barley unchanged, the excess demand for oats must also increase, as oats is a substitute for wheat. Since the total value of excess demands in terms of oats must remain at zero because of Walras' law, and since the values of the excess demands for barley and oats have increased, the value of the excess demand for wheat must have decreased. Given that the price of wheat has risen this means that the excess demand for wheat must have fallen when its price rose, so that wheat is normal.

Further, if there are only two commodities and both are normal then they must both be substitutes for each other. This is because an increase in the price of wheat in terms of oats is equivalent to a decrease in the price of oats in terms of wheat; since oats is normal this will result in a rise in the excess demand for oats, so that oats is a substitute for wheat. This in turn means that the economy must be representative, because if wheat is normal then its excess demand curve must be downward-sloping, so that equilibrium is unique; as shown in Section 9.4, this means that the economy is representative.

8. An economy with multiple markets must also be representative if all commodities are substitutes for each other, which means that any substitutive economy has a unique and stable equilibrium. However,

instead of using this indirect argument I shall demonstrate these properties directly. Before I do this it is worth noting that the simplifying assumption made in Section 9.5 is automatically satisfied if all commodities are normal, and thus if all commodities are substitutes for each other.

First note that in a substitutive economy the locus for wheat must be upward-sloping. If it had a downward-sloping segment this would mean that the excess demand for wheat remained unchanged at zero when the price of wheat increased and the price of barley decreased. This would be impossible, as both price changes would lead to an increase in the excess demand for wheat: the first because wheat is normal, and the second because wheat is a substitute for barley. In the same way we may see that the locus could not have a vertical or a horizontal segment.

Next, note that the locus for wheat can only intersect any given ray from the origine once. If it intersected such a ray twice, say, then the price of wheat in terms of barley would be the same at both intersection points, but the price of barley in terms of oats would be lower, and thus the price of oats in terms of barley would be higher, at the intersection point nearer to the origin; at the same time, the excess demand for wheat would remain unchanged at zero at both intersection points. This would be impossible as wheat is a substitute for oats.

Similarly, the locus for barley will be upward-sloping everywhere and only intersect any ray from the origin once. Thus the economy may be illustrated by the (solid) loci shown in Figure 11E. This demonstrates that equilibrium is unique; if it were not then at least one locus would have to recross the ray from the origin through the equilibrium combination nearest to the origin, that is the broken line in the figure. Since both loci are upward-sloping and equilibrium is unique it follows immediately from the argument of Section 10.6 that equilibrium is stable.

9. Figure 11E, in which the broken curve is the new locus for wheat, also confirms that in a substitutive economy the price of wheat must increase when there is an increase in the excess demand for wheat. In addition, this figure shows that the price of barley increases as well. Finally, this figure shows, that the new equilibrium combination μ must lie under the ray from the origin to the old equilibrium combination λ, which demonstrates that the price of wheat has increased proportionately more than the price of barley, or

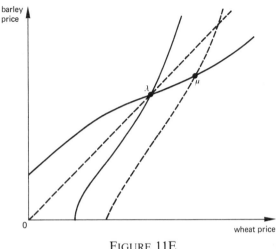

FIGURE 11E

equivalently that the price of wheat in terms of barley has risen.

These three results, that in a substitutive economy a shift in excess demand from oats to wheat leads to rises in the prices of wheat in terms of oats, of barley in terms of oats and of wheat in terms of barley, are known as the three Hicksian laws.

I shall conclude by considering what determines the extent to which prices change in response to a given shift in excess demand in substitutive economies.

The less the excess demand, and thus the demand, for barley responds to a change in the price of barley the steeper will be the locus for barley; in the extreme case where the demand for barley is not affected by the price of barley this locus will be vertical. On the other hand, the less the demand for barley responds to a change in the price of wheat the flatter will be the locus for barley; in the extreme case where the demand for barley is not affected by the price of wheat this locus will be horizontal. Thus the locus for barley becomes steeper as the demand for barley becomes either less responsive to the price of barley or more responsive to the price of wheat.

Now consider the effect of the original shift in excess demand from oats to wheat in two different economies: firstly in the original economy, and secondly in a modified economy, which is the original economy modified so that the demand for barley is either less responsive to changes in the price of barley or more responsive to changes in the price of wheat than in the original economy. This means that the locus for barley is steeper than in the original economy. So that these two economies are comparable the modification is such as to be compatible with the equilibrium of the original economy, in that the locus for barley in the modified economy intersects the (unchanged) locus for wheat at the original equilibrium.

This means that the locus for barley in the modified economy is below that in the original economy at all prices of wheat below the common equilibrium and above this at all prices of wheat above the common equilibrium. These two economies are illustrated in Figure 11F, where the flatter curve meeting the vertical axis is the locus for barley in the original economy, and the steeper such curve that for barley in the modified economy; the solid curve meeting the horizontal axis is the old locus for wheat in both economies, and the broken such curve the new locus for wheat in both economies. The old equilibrium in both economies is λ, the new equilibrium in the original economy is μ, and the new equilibrium in the modified economy is v. It is clear that the prices of both wheat and barley are higher at v than at μ, that is rise more in the modified economy than in the original

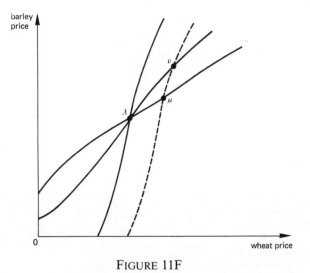

FIGURE 11F

These results, that in a substitutive economy the effect of a given shift in excess demand on all prices becomes greater when the demand for some commodity becomes either less responsive to changes in its own price or more responsive to changes in the prices of other commodities, are known as the fourth and fifth Hicksian laws.

12   Conclusion

1. The theory of value presented here may be summarised as follows. An economy consists of a number of agents, each of whom is endowed with some given amounts of various commodities and has some given preferences between these commodities. At any given prices each agent plans exchanges of commodities on the basis of these preferences and endowments; if all these planned exchanges are compatible then the prices are equilibrium prices, or values. Thus values are determined by agents' preferences and endowments, that is by scarcities.

This framework is well-defined. The definitions of commodities and of agents are coherent, and relate well to reality; given these definitions there are no problems in specifying planned exchanges, and when these are compatible.

Within this framework market equilibrium prices are generally accepted. Society as a whole accepts the market mechanism; provided that the economy is large all coalitions in society also accept this mechanism and all agents take market prices as given, though there may be some problems in small economies.

Equilibrium prices generally have satisfactory properties. Such prices always exist, and almost always depend continuously on the attributes of the economy; it is likely that these prices are unique, stable, and depend in a predictable way on the attributes of the economy, though these properties may not always apply.

2. This theory is one of value in exchange. I shall conclude by noting some implications of extending the theory to incorporate production, capital and money.

Perhaps the most obvious way in which the theory of exchange is an incomplete theory is that it abstracts from production, that is the transformation of some commodities into others, such as wheat into flour. We may introduce production into the theory by considering each agent to have, in addition to his preferences and endowment, some production technology. This is a specification of what production combinations, that is inputs and outputs, are feasible: for example, that it requires 2½ bushels of wheat to produce 1 hundred-weight of flour. At any given prices the profit from a production combination is the difference between the values of the outputs and inputs involved. Given some prices an agent now plans both a consumption bundle and a feasible production combination; these are such that the consumption bundle is the best, according to his preferences, of those available to him, that is those whose value is the same as that of his endowment together with the profit from his production combination.

The essential aspect of production follows from this: production and consumption plans are separable, in that an agent first plans the production combination which gives him the largest profit of those which are feasible, and then plans the best consumption bundle which is available given this profit. Thus an agent's production plan depends only on his technology, and not on his endowment or preferences (and thus, incidentally, not on his aversion to risk). An implication of this is that we may equally well consider production to be undertaken by 'firms', each with its own technology, in which agents have shares. Given this separation we may rework the various arguments justifying the focussing on equilibrium prices to incorporate production, and obtain essentially the same results.

Excess demands at any given price are now the difference between aggregate (consumption) demands and inputs into production on the one hand, and aggregate endowments and outputs of production on the other. Again these are related by Walras' law (although in fact Walras overlooked this in his discussion of production). Since the analysis of the properties of equilibrium prices is entirely in terms of excess demands we may immediately reinterpret this to incorporate production, and again obtain essentially the same results.

3. One of the more obvious aspects of production is that it may take time. In the simplest case flour today may be transformed into flour tomorrow, by storage. In this example flour is a capital good, that is a produced means of production. Its rate of return is the ratio of the value of the service it performs each day as a capital good to the value of the capital good itself, that is the ratio of the difference between the price of flour tomorrow and that of flour today to the price of flour today (assuming that storage is free). In a more interesting case flour tomorrow may be produced from labour today and wheat tomorrow by first transforming the labour into a mill, by building, and then

transforming the mill and wheat into flour (and, as a by-product, a used mill), by milling. In this case the mill is a capital good; its rate of return may be defined analogously to that of flour in the simpler example.

As commodities are distinguished by the time at which they are available this introduces no problems at a formal level, but it does invite a change of emphasis. One of the more important aspects to be recognised is that the rate of return of all capital goods actually used must be the same. In the above example if the rate of return of a mill were less than that of flour no agent would use labour to produce a mill, but would instead exchange labour for flour and then store this flour. This equality of rates of return leads the theory to focus on the explanation of this common rate of return, or the rates of profit, interest and growth.

4. A further way in which the theory of exchange is an incomplete theory is that it abstracts from money, that is an intrinsically worthless medium of exchange, such as pound notes. Exchange without money may be cumbersome, and involve an agent who plans to exchange oats for wheat finding one agent who both wants to acquire oats and surrender wheat. With money, however, he need only find some agent who plans to buy oats (that is exchange money for oats) and some, usually different, agent who plans to sell wheat (that is exchange wheat for money).

The essential aspect of money (or rather economies in which all exchanges must be for money) follows from this: an agent who plans to exchange oats for wheat must sell his oats before he can buy wheat (unless he has a sufficient reserve of money), and if he cannot sell his oats then he cannot buy wheat. Thus planned demands only become effective if they are backed up by money. This may lead to problems.

Consider an economy in which Leon is endowed with wheat only and Karl with oats only (and Maynard is endowed with barley and money), and where preferences have the usual properties (except that Maynard dislikes wheat and oats). At some given prices Leon may plan to sell oats and buy wheat, and Karl may plan to sell wheat and buy oats (while Maynard plans no exchanges). However, Leon will not be able to sell his oats as Karl has no money (and Maynard does not like oats), so his planned demand for wheat cannot become effective, and Karl is in a similar position. Thus effective excess demands for all commodities will be zero, and prices will not change, even though no planned exchanges can be made and there may be substantial planned excess demands. We therefore have a state of chronic planned, or true, excess demands, or of chronic disequilibrium.

Even if all planned exchanges can be made equilibrium may be highly volatile. This is because Leon, say, only accepts intrinsically worthless money in exchange for oats because he expects that he will be able to exchange this money for wheat. Thus agents only accept money because they expect other agents to do the same: any initial loss of confidence in money may have explosive effects.

5. To summarise, the incorporation of production and capital into the theory of value raises no fundamental problems. The incorporation of money raises a potential threat, but one which may well be empty (in the above example we should ask why agents do not agree to barter, why there is no borrowing and lending, and so forth). Focussing attention on disequilibrium rather than equilibrium outcomes takes us away from the microeconomic Walrasian paradigm, with its emphasis on value, and into the macroeconomic so-called Keynesian paradigm, with its emphasis on employment (since labour is usually taken to be the commodity in excess supply), and thus beyond the scope of our enquiry.

Appendix

My purpose in this book is to examine the relation between equilibrium price and scarcity, rather than to provide a justification for interpreting value as equilibrium price and thus establishing a relation between value and scarcity. However, I present a translation of Walras' discussion of this relationship in this appendix.

As a basis for this I have used Walras' *Abrege des Elements d'Economie Politique Pure*. This non-technical summary (published in 1938) was prepared by Walras from the material of the definitive edition of the *Elements* (published in 1926), and thus contains the final version of Walras' theory. Within each paragraph in this appendix nothing is omitted from the original other than some cross-references and examples, and nothing is added or changed.

The material is divided into two sections: Walras' Part I, which derives value from scarcity, and Walras' Part II, which completes the argument by deriving scarcity from value. The former is taken from Sections 21, 23, 24 and 28 of the original, and the latter from Sections 40, 41, 91, 92 and 93.

1. Social wealth comprises those tangible and intangible things (it does not matter which) that are scarce, that is both useful and available only in limited amounts.

Things are useful if they can serve any use at all, or satisfy some want. The distinction in ordinary language between the necessary, the useful, the agreeable and the superfluous is immaterial here; necessary, useful, agreeable and superfluous only mean more or less useful.

Things are available only in limited amounts if there is insufficient of them for everyone to satisfy his wants completely. There are various useful things which are available in unlimited amounts, but these are not scarce, and thus not a part of social wealth.

Useless things are not appropriated, for no-one would think of appropriating them. Useful things available in unlimited amounts are also not appropriated. Firstly, they cannot be controlled, for even if

99

someone wanted to withdraw them completely from the public domain he could not do so; and secondly, there would be little point in obtaining a small part of them and leaving the rest for everyone else.

On the other hand, useful things available in limited amounts are appropriable, and actually appropriated. Firstly, such things are controllable, in that it is possible for a number of individuals to obtain all of them, leaving none in the public domain. Secondly, such individuals gain a double advantage: they assure themselves of a guaranteed supply of these things to satisfy their wants, and also, if they do not want to consume all of them themselves, they may obtain other things which they do want to consume by exchanging their surplus for these.

Once scarce things have been appropriated (and they, and only they, can be appropriated) they have a special property relative to each other in addition to the utility they give, that of being exchangeable for each other. An individual who owns some scarce thing can obtain something else in exchange for it; if he does not own something he can obtain it only by exchanging something else for it, and if he has nothing to exchange he must go without. This is the concept of value in exchange.

Value in exchange, once established, is a natural concept, natural in its origin, its effects and its character. If wheat and silver have any value it is because they are scarce, that is useful and limited in availability, both natural properties. If wheat and silver have some given value relative to each other it is because they are relatively more or less scarce, that is more or less useful and limited in availability, the same two natural properties.

This does not mean that we cannot affect prices. Just because gravity is a natural concept and obeys natural laws it does not follow that we can only observe it. We may resist it or not, but we cannot change its character or its laws: only by obeying can we command. It is the same with value. In the case of wheat we could raise its price by destroying some of the supply or lower its price by eating something else in its stead; we could even fix its price by decree. In the first case we would be acting on the cause of value by substituting one natural value for another, and in the second we would be acting on value itself by substituting an artificial value for a natural one. We could even suppress value altogether by suppressing exchange, but if exchanges take place we cannot prevent them from determining values naturally, once demands and supplies, or scarcities, are given.

2. We defined social wealth earlier as comprising those tangible and

intangible things that are scarce, that is both useful and limited in availability, and showed that all, and only, such things have value. Here we shall proceed differently. We define social wealth as comprising those tangible and intangible things that have value, and show that all, and only, such things are useful and limited in availability. In the first case we proceeded from cause to effect, and in the second we proceed from effect to cause. Provided that we establish the connection between scarcity and value we may proceed in whichever direction we choose.

Value in exchange is a property which things have, not of being free, but of being bought and sold, that is acquired and surrendered in given amounts for other things. The buyer of something is the seller of the thing which he surrenders in exchange, while the seller of something is the buyer of the thing the acquires in exchange; thus all exchanges of two things for each other involve a double sale and a double purchase.

Things which have value in exchange are also known as commodities, the market being the environment in which commodities are exchanged. Value in exchange originates in the market and must be studied there. Value arises naturally in the market through competition: traders make their purchases by outbidding each other and their sales by underbidding each other, and this interaction determines the values of commodities, values which are somtimes rising, sometimes falling and sometimes stationary. The better competition functions the more precisely are values determined.

The exchange of two commodities for each other in a competitive market is an operation in which all holders of the commodities obtain the greatest satisfaction of their wants consistent with all purchases and sales being at the same rate of exchange.

If we define scarcity as the intensity of the last want satisfied we have the following proposition: market equilibrium prices are equal to the ratio of scarcities, or, in other words, values in exchange are proportional to scarcities.

We have now reached the objective of deriving scarcity from value in exchange instead of deriving value in exchange from scarcity. In fact scarcity defined here as the intensity of the last want satisfied is precisely the same as scarcity defined earlier by the twin conditions of usefulness and limitation of availability.

Given that scarcity and value in exchange are two proportional and concomitant phenomena it follows that scarcity is the cause of value.

Bibliography

This bibliography provides both references for works cited in the text and suggestions for further reading. Wherever possible the latter are surveys, which give an overview of the relevant area and in turn refer to more technical works themselves. However, even within this category the suggestions are selective rather than exhaustive.

The subject matter of many references is part of now 'common knowledge', and has been drawn on freely in the text without specific acknowledgement. All works from which more detailed arguments have been followed are identified by an asterisk.

References are divided into three section: works of now mainly historical interest, that is before Debreu's *Theory of Value*; more recent general works; and works specifically relating to the ten questions discussed in the text, subdivided accordingly.

1. HISTORICAL REFERENCES
Edgeworth, F. Y., *Mathematical Psychics* (London, 1881) Part II
Hicks, J. R., *Value and Capital* (Oxford, 1946; first published 1939) Part II
Pareto, V., *Manual of Political Economy* (New York, 1971; first published in Italian, 1906) chs III–VI
Schumpeter, J. A., *History of Economic Analysis* (London, 1954) Part IV
Wald, A., 'On Some Systems of Equations of Mathematical Economics', *Econometrica*, vol. 19 (1951; first published in German, 1936)
Walras, L., *Elements of Pure Economics* (London, 1954; first published in French, 1874; definitive edition, 1926; author's abridged version, *Abrege des Elements d'Economie Politique Pure,* 1938) Parts I–III

2. GENERAL REFERENCES
Allingham, M., *General Equilibrium* (London, 1975) chs 1–3, 5–7
Arrow, K. J. and Hahn, F. H., *General Competitive Analysis* (Edinburgh, 1971) chs 1–2, 4–12
Arrow, K. J. and Intrilligator, M. D. (eds), *Handbook of Mathematical Economics* (Amsterdam, 1982) chs 14–18
Debreu, G., *Theory of Value* (New York, 1959) chs 2, 4–7
Hildenbrand, W. and Kirman, A.P., *Introduction to Equilibrium Analysis* (Oxford, 1976) chs 1–2, 4–6
Malinvaud, E., *Lectures in Microeconomic Theory* (London, 1972; first published in French, 1969) chs 1–2, 4–5, 7, 11

3. SPECIFIC REFERENCES

Commodities: Debreu (chs 2, 7); Malinvaud (chs 1, 11)

Agents: Debreu (ch. 4); Malinvaud (ch. 2)

Society: Arrow and Hahn (ch. 4); Debreu (ch. 6)

Coalitions: Hildenbrand, W., 'Core of an Economy', ch. 18 in Arrow and Intrilligator; Hildenbrand and Kirman (chs 1, 5)

Price-Taking: Johansen, L., 'Price-Taking Behavior', *Econometrica*, vol. 45 (1977); Roberts, D. J. and Postlewaite, A., 'The Incentives for Price-Taking Behavior in Large Exchange Economies', *Econometrica*, vol. 44 (1976)*

Existence: Arrow and Hahn (chs 5–7); Debreu, G., 'Existence of Competitive Equilibrium', ch. 15 in Arrow and Intrilligator

Continuity: Debreu, G., 'The Application to Economics of Differential Topology and Global Analysis', *American Economic Review,* vol. 66 (1976); Shafer, W. and Sonnenschein, H., 'Market Demand and Excess Demand Functions', ch. 14 in Arrow and Intrilligator*

Uniqueness: Arrow and Hahn (ch. 9); Dierker, E., 'Regular Economies', ch. 17 in Arrow and Intrilligator

Stability: Arrow and Hahn (chs 11–12); Hahn, F. H., 'Stability', ch. 16 in Arrow and Intrilligator

Prediction: Allingham (ch. 7); Arrow and Hahn (ch. 10)

Index

Reference are to sections.

Agents
    defined, 3.2
    question, 3.1

Coalitions, *see* Core
Commodities
    bundles, 2.6
    contingent, 2.5
    defined, 2.2
    question, 2.1
Continuity
    non-critical economies, 8.5
    question, 8.1
Core
    approximation, 5.8
    defined, 5.2
    equal treatment, 5.6
    equilibria, and, 5.7
    examples, 5.3, 5.10, 5.11
    non-replicated economies, 5.9
    question, 5.1
Critical economies
    rareness, 8.6

Endowments
    defined, 3.10
Equilibria
    core, and, 5.4
    defined, 3.14
    example, 3.15
    optima, and, 4.5
Excess demands
    attributes, and, 8.2
    continuity in attributes, 8.3
    defined, 7.3
    example, 7.5
    inverse continuity, 8.4
    properties, 7.4

Exchanges
    contingent, 3.13
    example, 3.12
    planned, 3.11
Existence
    approximation, 7.12
    concave preferences, 7.9
    direct approach, 7.6
    examples, 7.8, 7.10
    indirect approach, 7.2
    large economies, 7.11
    linear preferences, 7.7
    non-replicated economies, 7.13
    question, 7.1

Indifference curves
    defined, 3.5
Manipulation
    defined, 6.2
    examples, 6.3, 6.4, 6.5, 6.10
    lacuna, 6.11
    non-replicated economies, 6.9
    question, 6.1
Multiple-Market economies
    defined, 9.5

Prediction
    defined, 11.2
    failure, 11.4
    multiple-market economies, 11.5
    non-representative economies,
      11.6
    question, 11.1
    representative economies, 113.
Preferences
    defined, 3.3
    example, 3.9
    properties, 3.4

scale-independent, 3.8
smooth, 3.7
Prices
defined, 2.3
Price-Taking, *see* Manipulation *and*
    Obtainable prices

Obtainable prices
approximation, 6.8
defined, 6.6
equilibria, and, 6.7
Optima
defined, 4.2
equilibria, and, 4.6
example, 4.8
incompletability of criterion, 4.3
incompleteness of criterion, 4.4
non-convex preferences, 4.9
question, 4.1
smooth preferences, 4.7
Replication
defined, 5.5
Representative economies
defined, 9.3

Society, *see* Optima
Stability
defined, 10.2
disequilibrium exchanges, 10.8
failure, 10.4
local, 10.7
multiple-market economies, 10.5

non-representative economies,
    10.6
question, 10.1
representative economies, 10.3
Substitutive economies
defined, 11.7
prediction, 11.9
uniqueness and stability, 11.8

Uncertainty
defined, 2.4
Uniqueness
multiple-market economies, 9.6
non-critical economies, 9.2
non-representative economies, 9.7
question, 9.1
representative economies, 9.4
Utilities
defined, 3.6

Value
assessment, 12.5
capital, and, 12.3
interpretation, 1.1
later developments, 1.4
money, and, 12.4
plan of the book, 1.5
production, and, 12.2
questions, 1.2
summary, 12.1
Walras' contribution, 1.3